AF493122

Game C++ Programming
A Practical Introduction
(Second Edition)
Kenwright

A practical introduction to writing and debugging C++ for real-time gaming environments (including programming examples, debugging tips, and good coding practices)

BOOK TITLE:
Game C++ Programming: A Practical Introduction
Second Edition
ISBN-13: 979-8-65-353109-5

Edition: 012062020

For information or any other inquiries, please contact:
apracticalintroduction@gmail.com

Table of Contents

Introduction and Overview

Imagination is more important than knowledge. For knowledge is limited to all we now know and understand, while imagination embraces the entire world, and all there ever will be to know and understand.

Albert Einstein

1.1 About this book

This book provides a beginner's introduction to C++ programming from a how-to perspective using practical examples and simple explanations. The book is written as a casual read rather than a technical reference manual. As you progress through the book, we outline warnings and good practices. This book is a 'practical' book - hence, it's recommended that you type in code samples and experiment. Try breaking the code and seeing what errors and warnings you get. Remember, curiosity fuels development.

1.2 The Journey Begins.....

Programming is an art. You don't become a great programmer overnight. Writing clear, concise, fast, straightforward code that is robust and tidy takes practice and time. You have to be patient. The main way in which you learn C++ is by writing lots of code in C++. This is true for every programming language as well.

But don't think that you can just read the whole book and then you'll know C++! You will forget most of the things you read unless you are reading while also coding. If you're a student, take a class that uses C++, set yourself small C++ projects. You'll hit difficult problems, there are many problems and unknowns when you start out but persistence is important. You'll write a lot of bad code. That's okay; as you learn more about the language, you can go back and rewrite your programs, but better. I recommend you just go for it - and have fun - don't worry about making mistakes.

Along the way, you'll have trouble. Sometimes you just won't know how to do something in C++. Now, you have two options. You can search around online for a solution, post a question on a forum, or you can just search for a snippet of code that does what you want and paste it into your program and adjust it until it works. You can find out what concept it is that you don't understand, and read articles which explain it, so you understand how to write the code properly for yourself. If you want to know C++ well, it goes without saying that you should do the latter!

Months or years pass. You've written thousands of lines of C++ code, and you generally have a good idea of how C++ works in most situations. But the language still makes frustratingly little sense. You still occasionally get error messages that are entire pages long. At this point, you'll want to really understand the nitty-gritty of C++. So what do you do? Read more books! Look in the 'Intermediate' and 'Advanced' articles and books. Tackle larger projects, forcing yourself to use even more parts of the language. Write a linked list or binary search tree class in C++ using templates, for example. Also, if you're ever curious about random things, like, if you have two overloads of a function, which one is going to get called, don't just be content to not know the answer. Open up your text editor and write a program and test which one gets called! If you don't understand why, then ask. And learn.

Never stop learning... and your knowledge will be bounded only by your life-span.

1.3 Why is Game Programming Different?

In retrospect, game programming isn't really different from other approaches, such as system and application development. You should always aim to write straightforward, computationally fast, and robust code in all your endeavours. However, cutting-edge high-end game engines are engineering accomplishment analogous to complete operating systems, such as Windows and Linux. Whereby, memory management, graphical output, physic simulations, and other system components are encompassed within the game engine. The majority of time, your code needs to run in real-time and needs to be able to recover from problems gracefully and quickly, while allowing the developer to fix the problem asap (e.g., asserts and log files).

1.4 Source Control (e.g., Repository Management - GIT and SVN)

While not really a programming matter, how you manage and store your code is important. For example, keeping track of source code changes, sharing code across multiple machines, and recording and identifying specific changes can make your life much easier. Additionally, it is an industry necessity.

You might feel like it is over-kill or one of those unneeded tasks, but it is definitely worth the effort. There are numerous free online repository management systems, such as, Bitbucket, Github, Sourceforce, that you can use to experiment with.

1.5 Limited Resources

The challenges can include systems with limited resources, such as, handheld devices like mobile phones. Writing code that is compact, bandwidth efficient, and computationally fast is crucial. So you need to understand what is happening. How memory is being allocated and moved around. Where the bottlenecks in your program are - is it a computational bottleneck or a memory limitation. You need to understand the problem so that you're able to identify the correct solution.

1.6 Road to Success

In the beginning, you'll be primarily struggling with learning syntax, basic programming principles, and structure. This can be straightforward, if time consuming and slow. Once you do master the basics, you'll move onto learning good programming ethics, algorithms, and optimisation tricks. This takes time. Experience is the road to writing well thought-out, structured, compact code. As you acquire a style and formatting preference - programming will become second-nature. Of course, just because you can write code easily, doesn't mean you are writing great code. You can get into bad habits easily. Persistence and an open mind are crucial. Being open minded means you'll improve and grow and become a successful developer in any language (see Figure 1.1).

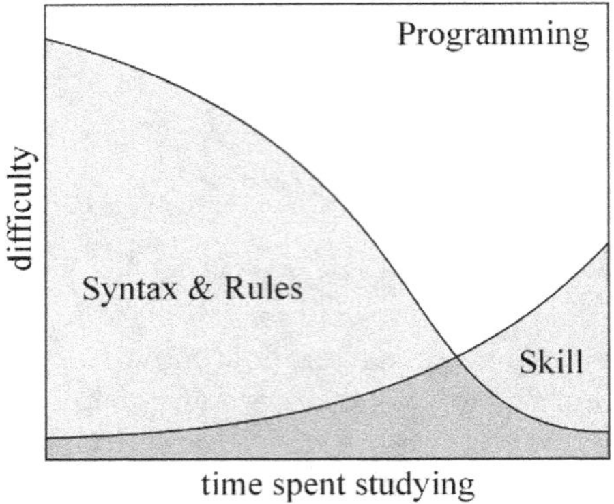

Figure 1.1. *Learning Graph - How your learning challenges will change over-time.*

1.7 Work Smarter Not Harder

Programming should not be a stressful and painful experience. There are a plethora of tools out there to help you. Don't be afraid to exploit them for profiling, debugging, and writing better code. Learn from others. Ask questions in forums, reverse engineering other peoples code, critically question 'why' things are done certain ways. The internet provides a wealth of resources at your fingertips.

1.7.1 A Colour Coded Editor (e.g., Notepad++ or Visual Studio)

Without a doubt a visual editor (e.g., notepad++ or Visual Studio) enables you to see at a glance, comments, keywords, and strings. You can write tidier, cleaner, more readable code. The days of small screen single colour displays has passed. We live in an era of high-definition multi-resolution wide-screen monitors.

```
#include<iostream>
using namespace std;
int main()
{   int palindrome, reverse=0;
    cout<<"Enter number:  ";
    cin>>palindrome;

    int num=0,key=palindrome;
            for(int i=1;palindrome!=0;i++){

                num=palindrome%10;
                palindrome=palindrome/10;
                reverse=num+(reverse*10);
            }
   if(reverse==key){
   cout<<key<<" is a Palindrome Number";
            }
            else{
   cout<<key<<"is NOT a Palindrome Number";
            }
return 0;
}
```

```
#include<iostream>
using namespace std;
int main()
{   int palindrome, reverse=0;
    cout<<"Enter number:  ";
    cin>>palindrome;

    int num=0,key=palindrome;
            for(int i=1;palindrome!=0;i++){

                num=palindrome%10;
                palindrome=palindrome/10;
                reverse=num+(reverse*10);
            }
   if(reverse==key){
   cout<<key<<" is a Palindrome Number";
            }
            else{
   cout<<key<<"is NOT a Palindrome Number";
            }
return 0;
}
```

Figure 1.2. ***Colour Coded Source Code*** - *Compare a simple colour editor output compared to black and white text (e.g., keywords, strings, and numbers stand out at a glance).*

1.7.2 Words That Change Colour

If you use an integrated development environment, such as Visual Studio, as you type, keywords, spelling errors, typing mistakes change colour or are underlined in the editor window in real-time, so you can catch and correct your mistakes while your creative juices are flowing.

1.8 Why Fix Warnings and Errors?

Well you need to fix errors because your code won't even compile, while warnings are typically dismissed and ignored by new developers. However, warnings are there to help you write better code. They can indicate any number of issues, for example, performance hits, such as converting between floats and double precision integers. Fix warnings! Don't ignore them. As warnings and errors arise, address the where and why and fix them.

1.9 Don't Be Afraid To Try New Things

What will happen? The code won't compile? The program will crash? The world won't end. However, exploring and experimenting will make you a more proficient and competent programmer. A programmer that has made a thousand mistakes has learned a thousand lessons (i.e., as long as the thousand mistakes aren't all the same mistake).

1.10 Trial and Error

Take a step back. Brute force trial and error can result in implementations that work by luck and not a solid understanding of what is happening. Leave the computer for an hour. Have a coffee. Talk to colleges about the problem. Jot down the problem on paper. Refreshed and full of ideals you'll write a better solution.

If the code you have written has syntax errors, the compiler will tell you. In the majority of cases, it will tell you what line and why it won't compile. If your algorithm logic has problems, it will crash or not work as you expected. However, the world will continue to spin, and you can rectify your mistake. So don't worry.

1.11 The Program Works The Same 'Every' Time (Not 'Sometimes')

Computers only do what you tell them to do. Programs should not run differently each time you run them (that is, in general cases). There should be no guessing or luck, if a program runs. These random random bugs are caused by a number of issues, such as, uninitialized variables or external input. A computer is a logical system, two plus two is always four - not sometimes four or five depending on how it feels.

1.12 Don't Assume - Know!

Never assume anything with software. If you know the value will always be between X and Y, then add a debug assert to verify this. Don't just think it will be correct. Know it! Add assert alerts to your code, so if your algorithm does produce impossible unforeseen values you'll be instantly alerted and can rectify the problem immediately.

1.13 Fast Isn't Fast Enough

In games, speed is important in games! If you make an algorithm twice as fast, a few weeks later, you'll be asked to make it even faster. When it comes to computational speed, fast isn't fast enough! However, a word of warning. Don't sacrifice reliability and readability for unnecessary minuscule gains in speed. Typically, smarter algorithms are much better than low-level optimisations, such as in-lining assembly language.

1.14 Initialization and Randomness

Unlike managed languages, such as Java and C#, variables are automatically initialized to some predefined state (i.e., typically zero). However, in C++ you have to do this yourself. Why? For one reason, speed. If you have millions of variables and they are all initialized it will cause a slowdown. You get to decide what is and isn't initialized and with what. Of course, if you forget to initialize a variable or assume it has some pre-defined value in it, you can end up with random effects, different each time you run the simulation. In some situations, you'll get warnings about uninitialized variables by the compiler, but not always, so be careful.

1.15 How Simple?

Experience, practice, revising, and editing produces clean, concise, well written code. As with great writing, it can take a great deal of editing and revising to make a complex piece of code elegant and beautiful. Be patient. Learn from others, search on the web, and try out new ideas.

1.16 Formatting and Indentation

Why squash all your code onto one line? It doesn't run any faster. It doesn't make it compile faster. For example, see Listing 1.1 below and compare it to Listing 1.2.

```
1  int main() {
2    B b; b.f(true);
3    b.f(1);
4      A* a = &b;
5      a->f(true);
6  return 0; }
```

Listing 1.1. Why squash code together? In the example, the indentation is all over the place, multiple operations on the same line, variables names are non-descriptive (i.e., a, b, and f), and no comments; leaving a person with no idea what on earth is going on.

```
1   int main()
2   {
3     // Simple counter class
4     Counter count;  // Create instance of counter class
5     count.Reset();  // Reset counter to zero
6     count.Add(2);   // Increment the counter by 2
7     Counter* refCount =
8       &count;       // Create a pointer to the counter class instance
9     count->Reset(); // Reset counter via pointer reference
10    return 0;       // Exit
11  }
```

Listing 1.2. Modified version of Listing 1.1 with comments and aligned indentation.

1.17 Why C++ and not C# or Java?

With great power comes great responsibility. As with most programming languages, if you don't write good code, of course it will do bad things, C++ especially. For example, you can cause your whole computer to crash.

As Bjarne Stroustrup (inventor of the C++ language) says, "C makes it easy to shoot yourself in the foot; C++ makes it harder, but when you do it blows your whole leg off."

Other languages don't offer you direct access to system resources. Managing memory and initialization of components for you. These managed higher level languages are often wrote in C and C++.

That being said, though, C++ is probably the least beginner-friendly out of all mainstream programming languages (C#, Java, Python). Because of its complexity, it takes a long time to develop a good mental model of C++.

Essentially, C++ is an industry standard that provides enormous flexibility and power.

1.18 Lower-Case and Upper-Case

C++ is a case-sensitive language. So a variable called "CAT" isn't the same as a variable called "cat" (for example, see Listing 1.3).

```
1   int cat;
2   int Cat;
3   int cAT;
4   int CAT;
```

Listing 1.3. Case-sensitive example, each of the variables are different.

1.19 Comments? Too Much? Why Comment?

Comments are helpful. A few lines of in-line comments can make a complex optimized algorithm make sense. Comments make your code more readable and clearer, both to others and yourself. Putting your source code into words also helps you clarify the meaning in your head behind a function or algorithm. If you understand how your code is working sufficiently, you should be able to explain it simply to another developer. If you can't explain how it works, you don't understand how it works.

1.20 Naming Conventions (m Underscore?)

1.20.1 Old Naming Trends (Are They Necessary?)

Are naming conventions old fashioned? Have visual editors made it unnecessary to name variables in a specific convention so that we can easily identify what type it's at a glance? There is much debate as to what is a good or bad naming convention. However, consistency is important. Don't write some parts of your code using one style and other parts in other styles. Always look at your code from a third person perspective and ask yourself, is that algorithm or code transparently clear - and if not, why?.

Initially, hungarian notation was a popular choice for developers - originating from early C compilers. This was important because compilers were not able to give warnings or identify flawed indirections. People who are fluent in other high level languages, such as, C#, are always shocked when they see variables named using hungarian notation, an example is shown in Listing 1.4.

However, when maintaining legacy code that does follow some conventions consistently (even if loosely), you should stick to the conventions used there - at least in the existing modules / compilation units to be maintained.

```
1  struct MyStruct
2  {
3     TCHAR            szMyChar[STRING_SIZE];
4     bool             bMyBool;
5     unsigned long    ulMyLong;
6     void*            pMyPointer;
7     MyObject**       ppMyObjects;
8  }
```

Listing 1.4. Full hungarian naming convention.

1.20.2 Naming Functions, Variables, And Classes

Over time, you'll develop your own style that fit you. Alternatively, if you work for a company, you'll be forced to adopt theirs. Either way, a consistent well thought out naming convention can make your code more readable and cleaner. Both for yourself and others. For example, always starting function names with a capital letter and variable names with a lower case letter.

1.21 Most Importantly, Have Fun

As you take the programming adventure remember to have fun. After all, You are programming for games, and games are fun, right?

Also let other people see your code - be open minded, write mini games, push yourself and don't give up. Becoming a great programmer takes time - and it usually involves learning from others. Locking yourself in a room learning C++ by yourself will give you a good understanding of the language - however, letting other people see your code and getting it reviewed - will make you a better at programmer. Don't be afraid of criticism. Most programmers know what it's like to learn programming for the first time - their first hello world program. There are a lot of experts who are willing to give good advice on improving your code. Don't get disheartened. It takes some time and patience but you will get there.

Keep pushing forwards...

Chapter 2

Basics C++ (Once Upon A Time...)

With great power comes great responsibility.

Stan Lee - Spiderman

2.1 Computers Only Do What You Tell Them

We haven't reached the days of true artificial intelligence (i.e., self thinking smart computers). We can't tell our computer what we want and expect it to fill in all the gaps and details and give us an answer we want. That day isn't here yet! We need to give a computer explicit instructions to accomplish any task. Higher level languages, such as, C++, allow us to use pre-written libraries to accomplish more in a shorter time. However, computers are just machines that follow instructions step-by-step.

2.2 What Is A Function (Or Method)?

Quite simply, a function (also sometimes called a method) is an command. You command the computer do perform an operation, e.g., draw a line or put some text on screen. A program can be as simple as adding two numbers or as complex as a whole computer game. A function can call other functions, and these functions can call further functions (e.g., a hierarchical interconnected set of commands). Hence, other developers create algorithms and functions hidden away in libraries that are available to you by means of simple function calls. Think of functions as building blocks. You connect them together to achieve some specific task. Some of the blocks can be your own. Some can be borrowed (i.e., common pre-built libraries).

2.3 main() - The Journey Begins

The start of 'all' your programs begins at the 'main' function. You only have one 'main' function. For example, if you have dozens or hundreds of functions scattered across many files how do you know where to begin? Look for the program entry point, that is, the 'main' function. From there everything begins. When you run your program the system searches for the entry point 'main'. From there you decide what functions do and don't get called and in what order. Hypothetically, you could put your whole game code in a single function called main, but that would just be dirty!

2.4 How To Compile Your Program? (Visual Studio)

While you can type your program in any basic text editor (e.g., notepad++), you still need some way of compiling your program. Rather than keep your editor and compiler separate, use an integrated development environment (IDE) (e.g., Visual Studio) which will manage all your files and allow you to easily change and run your program with the press of a key. Furthermore, the IDE has all the bells and whistles, for example, colour coding, spell-checking, and optimisation profiling.

As a side note - if you are using the Microsoft C/C++ Compiler (cl.exe which will be in a subdirectory of your Visual Studio installation), open the Visual Studio command prompt (it will have appropriate paths set). In order to compile a file called "hello.cpp", type:

```
1    cl.exe hello.cpp
```

2.5 Hello World - Tradition...

Your first program should output 'hello world'. It's tradition. Since the dawn of computers. You are following the steps of every new programmer. Hence, power up the compiler, create an empty text file called 'hello.cpp' and type in Listing 2.1. If you typed it in 'exactly', it should compile without any warnings or errors and spit out 'hello world' on the screen.

```
1  #include <stdio.h>          // We need this so we can use 'printf'
2  void main()                 // Program entry point!
3  {
4    printf("hello world");    // Print string on screen
5  }                           // End program  .
```

Listing 2.1. Your first program (i.e., hello.cpp) - hello world

2.5.1 Why Won't It Work?

If your first program didn't compile. You didn't type Listing 2.1 in exactly? For example, did you include the semi-colon at the end of the printf? As it's essential not optional for your program to compile correctly.

2.5.2 How Do We Call Other Functions?

You call a function with its name followed by a pair of brackets. For example, in Listing 2.1 you call the function 'printf' which is another function declared within an external library. We can put parameters that we want to pass to the function within the bracket after the function name.

2.6 .h and .cpp ??

You need to know about the two types of C++ file types, i.e., '.h' and '.cpp'. Your implementation code (i.e., the real meat and potatoes) goes in the .cpp files. The .h files are for definitions. Typically, .h and .cpp files come in pairs (e.g., hello.h and hello.cpp).

So what do we mean by implementations and definitions? The implementation is the actual code that performs the real work, while the definition is details, such as the function name and its parameter list.

The principle behind the separate the separate header files (.h) and implementation files (.cpp) is a function cannot be called without first being declared. For example, if we have two functions, called 'main' and 'cat' shown below in Listing 2.2 and we try and call the function 'cat' from 'main' we get a compile error. Why? This is because the compile goes line-by-line down the file. When we reach the line to call the function 'cat' it hasn't heard anything about 'cat' yet so it stops and gives an error.

```
1   #include <stdio.h>         // We need this so we can use 'printf'
2   void main()                // Program entry point!
3   {
4      cat();          // Won't work?  What is this?  Why?
5   }
6
7   void cat()           // Simple function when called prints out "cat"
8   {
9      printf("cat");
10  }
```

Listing 2.2. Line by line from the top of the program. Hence, calling a function before the compiler has come across it will trigger a compile error. (This source code won't compile).

The solution to fix the error above shown in Listing 2.2 is to do a forward declaration (i.e., put the function name at the top of the file so the compiler knows about the function). This is shown below in Listing 2.3 and will compile and work.

```
1
2   void cat();          // ***Forward declaration of function cat***
3
4   #include <stdio.h>         // We need this so we can use 'printf'
5   void main()                // Program entry point!
6   {
7      cat();          // Won't work?  What is this?  Why?
8   }
9
10  void cat()           // Simple function when called prints out "cat"
11  {
12     printf("cat");
13  }
```

Listing 2.3. Line by line from the top of the program. Hence, calling a function before the compiler has come across it will trigger a compile error. (This source code won't compile).

As programs get larger and you have many functions being called from different files it's inefficient to go putting all the forward declarations at the top of each file. Instead, you put them all in header files (.h). You can then place them at the top of your file using the '#include' command, shown in Listing 2.4 and Listing 2.5.

```
1   // cat.h
2   void cat();          // ***Forward declaration of function cat***
```

Listing 2.4. Declaration file (cat.h).

```
1   // cat.cpp
2   #include "cat.h"         // ***Include our header file (cat.h)***
3
4   #include <stdio.h>           // We need this so we can use 'printf'
5   void main()                  // Program entry point!
6   {
7     cat();              // Won't work?  What is this?  Why?
8   }
9
10  void cat()            // Simple function when called prints out "cat"
11  {
12    printf("cat");
13  }
```

Listing 2.5. Include header file (cat.h) at the top of the file. Same as placing all the contents of the cat.h at this location.

2.7 *#include*

The '#include' command is a macro. Macros are pre-processed before the compiler begins. The '#include' macro searches for the specified file and replaced the contents of the file at the location of the #include line.

2.8 Don't Put Code In The *.h*!

As you start to master C++, you might be tempted to put code in the .h file. I mean the actual function implementation code in the .h. It might even work (initially). Since an '#include' copies the contents of the .h file into the .cpp file then compiles it. However, it's bad!! I know it can be tempting. It can be so easy to type the code in the .h file. Just don't do it! When you start using multiple 'includes' for files, and your project gets larger, it won't work. You'll get errors. Remember to put your implementation code in the .cpp file.

2.9 externs

Externs come in handy when you are working with global variables and functions. You declare the existence of the global variable or function so the the source file knows about it, but you only need to 'define' it once in that file.

For example, using 'extern int x;' tells the compiler that an object of type int called x exists somewhere. It's not the compilers job to know where it exists, it just needs to know the type and name so it knows how to use it.

Once all of the source files have been compiled, the linker will resolve all of the references of x to the one definition that it finds in one of the compiled source files. For it to work, the definition of the x variable needs to have what's called 'external linkage', which basically means that it needs to be declared outside of a function (at what's usually called 'the file scope') and without the static keyword.

2.10 Definition & Declaration

A **declaration** introduces an identifier and describes its type, be it a type, object, or function. A declaration is what the compiler needs to accept references to that identifier. These are declarations:

```
1  extern int bar;
2  extern int g(int, int);
3  double f(double, int); // extern can be omitted for function ↵
       declarations
4  class foo; // no extern allowed for class
```

A **definition** actually instantiates/implements this identifier. It's what the linker needs in order to link references to those entities. These are definitions corresponding to the above declarations:

```
1  int bar;
2  int g(int lhs, int rhs) {return lhs*rhs;}
3  double f(double d, int i) {return i+d;}
4  class foo {};
```

You are unable to use a variable or call a function in your code until you have defined it - either using a definition or a declaration. A definition can be used in the place of a declaration. An identifier can be declared as often as you want. Thus, the following is legal in C and C++:

```
1  double f(int, double);
2  double f(int, double);
3  extern double f(int, double); // the same as the two above
4  extern double f(int, double);
```

However, it must be defined exactly once. If you forget to define something that's been declared and referenced somewhere, then the linker doesn't know what to link references to and complains about a missing symbols. If you define something more than once, then the linker doesn't know which of the definitions to link references to and complains about duplicated symbols.

> **Declaration:** "Somewhere, there exists a snoopy" (snoopy is a function or variable and we can do as many declarations as we want).

Definition: "...and here it is!" (must only be done once).

2.11 What Is A Variable? (The Basics)

Variables in a computer program are analogous to "Buckets" or "Envelopes" where information can be maintained and referenced. On the outside of the bucket is a name. When referring to the bucket, we use the name of the bucket, not the data stored in the bucket.

```
1  int     apple;  // integer variable called 'apple'
2  float   cat;       // decimal point variable called 'cat'
3  double  mouse;    // double precision variable called 'mouse'
4  char*   myarray = "cat"; // string of characters called 'cat'
```

Listing 2.6. Variable Examples.

Variables are 'Symbolic Names'. This means the variable 'stands in' for any possible values. This is similar to mathematics, where it is always true that if given two positive numbers (lets use the symbols 'a' and 'b' to represent them):

```
1  a + b > a
```

Listing 2.7. Add any two numbers, the sum is greater than one of the numbers by itself.

This is called Symbolic Expression, again meaning, when any possible (valid) values are used in place of the variables, the expression is still true.

2.11.1 What can we do with Variables?

There are only a few things you can do with a variable:

- Create one (with a nice name).
  A variable should be named to represent all possible values that it might contain. Some examples are: myscore, myscores, mypoints, and myname.
- Put some information into it (destroying whatever was there before).
- We 'put' information into a variable using the assignment operator (=), e.g., myscore = 93;   (note - don't get confused with the boolean equality operator ==).
- Get a copy of the information out of it (leaving a copy inside)
  We 'get' the information out by simply writing the name of the variable, the computer does the rest for us, e.g., totalval = (myval1 + myval2) / 2.

2.12 Understanding Strings

A string is just an array of characters. Each character is one byte each. We identify the 'end' of the string using a 'null' character. For example, an ascii string containing the word "hippo" would be SIX characters in memory not five, due to the additional null terminating character. When we use double quotes (") in C++ it automatically converts the string to an array of characters in memory with a null terminating character. We using a single quote (') to list individual characters. For example:

```
1  char* a = "h"; // two characters in memory
2  char  b = 'h'; // single character in memory
```

Remember, double quotes (") returns a pointer to the location in memory of the first array element, while single quotes (') returns the value of the ascii character. We review character strings further when we discuss memory management in Section 7.9.2 (introducing further concepts, such as, unicode instead of ascii strings for additional languages).

Decimal	Hex	Char	Decimal	Hex	Char	Decimal	Hex	Char	Decimal	Hex	Char
0	0	[NULL]	32	20	[SPACE]	64	40	@	96	60	`
1	1	[START OF HEADING]	33	21	!	65	41	A	97	61	a
2	2	[START OF TEXT]	34	22	"	66	42	B	98	62	b
3	3	[END OF TEXT]	35	23	#	67	43	C	99	63	c
4	4	[END OF TRANSMISSION]	36	24	$	68	44	D	100	64	d
5	5	[ENQUIRY]	37	25	%	69	45	E	101	65	e
6	6	[ACKNOWLEDGE]	38	26	&	70	46	F	102	66	f
7	7	[BELL]	39	27	'	71	47	G	103	67	g
8	8	[BACKSPACE]	40	28	(	72	48	H	104	68	h
9	9	[HORIZONTAL TAB]	41	29	)	73	49	I	105	69	i
10	A	[LINE FEED]	42	2A	*	74	4A	J	106	6A	j
11	B	[VERTICAL TAB]	43	2B	+	75	4B	K	107	6B	k
12	C	[FORM FEED]	44	2C	,	76	4C	L	108	6C	l
13	D	[CARRIAGE RETURN]	45	2D	-	77	4D	M	109	6D	m
14	E	[SHIFT OUT]	46	2E	.	78	4E	N	110	6E	n
15	F	[SHIFT IN]	47	2F	/	79	4F	O	111	6F	o
16	10	[DATA LINK ESCAPE]	48	30	0	80	50	P	112	70	p
17	11	[DEVICE CONTROL 1]	49	31	1	81	51	Q	113	71	q
18	12	[DEVICE CONTROL 2]	50	32	2	82	52	R	114	72	r
19	13	[DEVICE CONTROL 3]	51	33	3	83	53	S	115	73	s
20	14	[DEVICE CONTROL 4]	52	34	4	84	54	T	116	74	t
21	15	[NEGATIVE ACKNOWLEDGE]	53	35	5	85	55	U	117	75	u
22	16	[SYNCHRONOUS IDLE]	54	36	6	86	56	V	118	76	v
23	17	[ENG OF TRANS. BLOCK]	55	37	7	87	57	W	119	77	w
24	18	[CANCEL]	56	38	8	88	58	X	120	78	x
25	19	[END OF MEDIUM]	57	39	9	89	59	Y	121	79	y
26	1A	[SUBSTITUTE]	58	3A	:	90	5A	Z	122	7A	z
27	1B	[ESCAPE]	59	3B	;	91	5B	[	123	7B	{
28	1C	[FILE SEPARATOR]	60	3C	<	92	5C	\	124	7C		
29	1D	[GROUP SEPARATOR]	61	3D	=	93	5D	]	125	7D	}
30	1E	[RECORD SEPARATOR]	62	3E	>	94	5E	^	126	7E	~
31	1F	[UNIT SEPARATOR]	63	3F	?	95	5F	_	127	7F	[DEL]

Figure 2.1. *Ascii Table* - *We store character strings in memory using numbers. The character 'a' in memory is stored as 97 decimal.*

```
1  char    singleCharA = 'a';
2  char    singleCharB = 'b';
```

```
3   char* myarray      = "cat";
4   // myarray[0] == 'c'
5   // myarray[1] == 'a'
6   // myarray[2] == 't'
7   // myarray[3] == '\0'
```

Listing 2.8. Variable Examples.

Things to remember:

- a string always terminates with a null character (e.g., the length of "cat" is four not three bytes)
- the variable points to the address of the first byte of the array of characters
- the double quotes around "cat" (e.g., Listing 2.8) and Hello World, are "constant strings" of characters.

2.12.1 Silly String Mistakes

When you start out with programming, especially if you've come from a managed language, such as Java, you need to be aware that string operations are at a low-level. For example, manipulation and comparison are done byte-by-byte.

For example, if we have two string arrays of different length (e.g., char* stringA="abc"; char* stringB="defg"), some things to be aware of:

- comparison - "stringA == stringB"!! bad bad bad - and will only compare the first two memory address bytes and note each element of the string array
- copying - "stringA = stringB" !!! no no no - you can't copy a string this way. Since this will only only copy the address not the string items. Furthermore, be warned that the string lengths are different, so if you copy byte-by-byte, the new string has to be the same length or longer in memory to ensure you don't go overwriting memory and causing corruption.

2.13 Displaying Strings With *printf* (e.g., *dprintf* - What Is The '%' Sign For?)

We touched upon 'print' in the hello world example. However, we didn't go into details, such as, how printf works, and how to format the string. For instance, what if we want to display an integer, string, or a double. We accomplish this using the special percent character '%'.

```
1  dprintf("%c", 'a');     // print single character 'a'
2  dprintf("%s", "cat");   // print string characters
3  dprintf("%d", 10);      // print integer 10
4  dprintf("0x%x", 16);    // print integer 16 out in hex format
```

Listing 2.9. Printf Paramater Example.

Specifics:

- "\n" - insert new line
- "\t" - insert a tab
- "\%" - string insert '\%' followed by the type, e.g., c(character), s(string), d(integer), f(float).

Remember, you can mix the string formatting command (i.e., '\%') with padding information, such as decimal places, left/right alignment, and trailing or leading spaces.

2.14 What About 'cout' and 'cin'? More Object Orientated?

In practice, games written in C++ don't use cout and cin. (e.g., game debug output). However, the C++ standard has two popular input/output functions, called, *cin* and *cout*.

2.14.1 cout

So by default, the standard output of a program points at the screen. So with the cout operator and the "insertion" operator (<<) you can print a message onto the screen. For example, see Listing 2.10.

```
1  #include<iostream>
2  using namespace std;
3  int main()
4  {
5    cout << "Hello World";
6    cout << 'y';
7    cout << 22;
8    return 0;
9  }
```

Listing 2.10. Standard Cout Example. (Notice, you don't need to specify the output format as you do with dprintf).

2.14.2 cin

While in most cases the standard input device is the keyboard, the cin and "$>>$" operator make it possible to take the input from the keyboard and put it in a variable. For example, see Listing 2.11.

```cpp
#include<iostream>
using namespace std;
int main()
{
   char achar;
   cout << "Press a key and press return: ";
   cin  >> achar;
   cout << achar;
   return 0;

}
```

Listing 2.11. Standard Cin Example. (Notice, you don't need to specify the output format as you do with scanf).

Notes:

- The cin and cout operator are chainable (e.g., cin $>>$ a $>>$ b;)
- Also mix in newline and tab operators (e.g., '\n' and '\t')

2.15 Other Input Output Methods

While the basic 'printf', 'cin', and 'cout' are common methods of inputting and outputting to the screen and keyboard. We can additionally, input and output to files.

2.15.1 Input (Opposite of printf, i.e., scanf)

```c
#include<stdio.h>
int main()
{
   int anum;
   scanf("%d", &anum);
   if ( 10 == mynumber )
   {
     printf("Is equal\n");
   }
   return 0;
}
```

Listing 2.12. An example of reading in a value from the keybaord using scanf.

2.15.2 File Input Output(i.e., fopen, fclose, fscanf, and fprintf)

You can read and write to files using three simple standard C libraries:

- *fopen* - takes the name of filename and returns a file handle that we use to read or write to the file
- *fclose* - closes the opened file (takes the opened file handle returned from *fopen*)
- *fprintf* - analogous to *printf*, except it takes a file handle and redirects the output to the file instead of the standard output
- *fscanf* - same as *scanf* for reading in text from the keyboard, however, it takes the file handle and reads from the open file

A simple file access example is shown in Listing 2.13.

```
1   #include<stdio.h>
2   int main()
3   {
4     // Create and open a txt file called op.txt
5     FILE* fp = fopen("op.txt", "wt");
6     // The returned variable value we call 'fp'
7     // is a handle we use to write to that file
8
9     // Next we write some strings and numbes to the file
10    fprintf(fp,"%s\n",    "test");
11    fprintf(fp,"%d\n",    20);
12
13    // Close the file and we are finished
14    fclose(fp);
15
16    // Null the pointer, just so it can't be used - good practice
17    fp = NULL;
18
19    return  0;
20  }// End main(..)
```

Listing 2.13. An example of reading in a value from the keybaord using scanf.

2.16 Summary

This chapter has briefly covered an enormous amount of information in a short amount of time to get your rolling. Concepts, such as, functions, strings, and file organisation - which, while you may be able to use you don't yet really understand. As we progress through the book - we'll go into further detail on each of these topics gain to allow you to gain a more in-depth understanding.

Chapter 3

Deeper Understanding

Any intelligent fool can make things bigger, more complex, and more violent. It takes a touch of genius – and a lot of courage – to move in the opposite direction.

Albert Einstein

3.1 Memory and Variables

This chapter explains the principle of memory and variables. With any algorithm or program you are manipulating and moving memory about to accomplish a specific task. Rather than remembering exact memory addresses, we give the memory addresses names, known as variables. For example:

```
1   int a = 10;
```

Places the value 10 in variable 'a'. Variable 'a' is a virtual name for an address in memory that we can use instead of the specific address. When compiled the compiler would associate the variable 'a' with a specific memory location.

3.2 References '&'

The special character '&' is used for two purposes:

- to 'link' or reference multiple variable names to the same memory location.
- to obtain the actual real address of the variable

```
1  // Referencing two variables
2  int  a = 22;
3  int &b = a;
4
5  b = 2; // This will change 'a' to 2, since variable 'b' references ←
          variable 'a'.  Basically, they both point to the same memory.
```

Listing 3.1. Referencing same memory with multiple variable names.

```
1  int a = 22;
2  int b = &a;  // Get the memory location of variable 'a' and put it in←
          variable 'b'.
3
4  // Both print the same value - i.e., the memory location of variable←
          'a'.
5  printf("address of a is: 0x0X", &a);
6  printf("address of a is: 0x0X", b); // e.g. 0x02B72399
```

Listing 3.2. Reference operator to return the memory location the variable stores the values.

3.3 Fundamental Variables

Variables are not all equal. Different variables take up different space in memory. For example, a 'char' variable uses 1 byte, while an 'float' variable uses 4 bytes.

- char   - 1 byte
- short   - 2 bytes
- int   - 4 bytes
- float   - 4 bytes
- double - 8 bytes

However, if that wasn't enough, we also have 'signed' and 'unsigned' for additional variable control. For example, a 'signed int' uses the first 'bit' of the four bytes of the variable for the sign of the value (i.e., 0 for negative and 1 for positive).

```
1  int            a = -1;
2  unsigned int   b = 44;
3  char           c = 22;
```

```
4   unsigned char d = 23;
```

If you don't specify 'signed' or 'unsigned', the variable defaults to 'signed'.

3.3.1 boolean, integers, floats, doubles

Understand the differences between the different variables. For example, you can put a 'float' into an 'int', but at a cost, both computational cycles and decimal accuracy should be taken into consideration.

A 'unsigned short' variable is of size 2 bytes. Hence, it can have 2^{16} different combinations. Therefore, you can only store values between 0 and 16384. You can't store values greater than this. In most circumstances the compiler will let you put larger numbers in the variable but will be stored incorrectly.

3.4 Casting - changing type

Typically, if we try and put a variable with greater precision into a variable with less precision (e.g., 4-byte integer into a 1-byte char) the compiler will give a warning:

```
1   char a = 10;
2   int  b = 22;
3        a = b;   // ***Warning** - Putting 4-byte int into a 1-byte char
```

We can force 'cast' one type of variable into another using 'brackets'. For example:

```
1   char a = 10;
2   int  b = 22;
3        a = (char)b;   // Cast 'b' into char
```

Be warned though - with great power comes great responsibility. If you are casting from one type to another be sure you understand what will be lost, since the compiler will not warn or notify you. Furthermore, the computational cost of converting a variable from one type to another will still be done, even though you won't be told about with.

3.5 Why Double Precision? (i.e., *float* Or *double*)

With modern computers most internal calculations are done with 'double' precision decimal place maths. This means each math variable uses 8-bytes and can produce highly accurate and precise calculations.

Nevertheless, it can be costly if you have large numbers of variables. For example, if you are storing and rendering a complex 3D geometric object, the 3D object can take millions of values. In terms of memory it can be expensive to store and be unnecessary to store in double precision. Typically, a 4-byte float precision variable is enough.

In games and graphics 'floats' are the default variable.

3.6 *sizeof*

At any moment, we might need to know how large a variable, structure, or class might be. For memory allocation or calculations. This can be accomplished using the *sizeof* function, as shown below in Listing 3.6:

```
int     a = 2;
short   k = 22;
double  p = 2.0;

printf("sizeof: %d \n", sizeof(a) );   // will print 4
printf("sizeof: %d \n", sizeof(k) );   // will print 2
printf("sizeof: %d \n", sizeof(p) );   // will print 8
```

3.7 Number Wrapping

As mentioned variables have number limits. For example, if we have an unsigned char, its range is from 0 to 255. If we place 255 in it, then increment it by 1, the variable will indicate it has 0 in it:

```
unsigned char a = 255;
printf("a: %d \n", a );   // prints 255
a = a + 1;                // add 1 to variable
printf("a: %d \n", a );   // prints 0
```

This is very important if you try and put values in variables that are in excess of the variable limits. Take caution!

If possible write your code so that it asserts if values exceed or go outside acceptable ranges.

3.8 *typedef* (Tidier Code)

We can write more organized and readable code by exploiting the 'typedef' operator. Essentially, replacing variable definitions with simpler more concise ones:

```
typedef unsigned int   uint32;
typedef unsigned char  uchar8;
typedef int            int32;
typedef unsigned char  byte;

int32 a = 22;  // same as writing unsigned int a = 22;
byte  b = 9;   // same as writing unsigned char b = 9;
```

3.9 Unions & Structs - making better use of memory variable organisation

You wrap variables inside a '*struct*' or '*union*' to accomplish a specific task. Essentially, a '*struct*' uses all the memory of its member and a '*union*' uses the largest members memory space.

With a *union*, you're only supposed to use one of the elements, because they're all stored at the same spot. This makes it useful when you want to store something that could be one of several types. A *struct*, on the other hand, has a separate memory location for each of its elements and they can all be used at once.

To give a concrete example of their use, if you're working on a program that overlays data types using the C/C++ language. This involved storing in your data in a *struct* and an *enum* indicating the type of value and a union to store that value. For example:

```
union foo {
int a;    // can't use both a and b at once
char b;
} foo;

struct bar {
int a;    // can use both a and b simultaneously
char b;
} bar;

union foo x;
x.a = 3; // OK
x.b = 'c'; // NO! this affects the value of x.a!

struct bar y;
y.a = 3; // OK
y.b = 'c'; // OK
```

If you're wondering what setting *x.b* to 'c' changes the value of *x.a* to, technically speaking it's undefined. On most modern machines a *char* is 1 byte and an *int* is 4 bytes, so giving *x.b* the value 'c' also gives the first byte of *x.a* that same value:

```
union foo x;
x.a = 3;
x.b = 'c';
printf("%i, %i\n", x.a, x.b);
prints

99, 99
Why are the two values the same? Because the last 3 bytes of the int
    3 are all zero, so it's also read as 99. If we put in a larger
    number for x.a, you'll see that this is not always the case:

union foo x;
x.a = 387439;
x.b = 'c';
printf("%i, %i\n", x.a, x.b);
prints

387427, 99
```

To get a closer look at the actual memory values, let's set and print out the values in hex:

```
union foo x;
x.a = 0xDEADBEEF;
x.b = 0x22;
printf("%x, %x\n", x.a, x.b);
prints

deadbe22, 22
```

You can clearly see where the $0x22$ overwrote the $0xEF$.

BUT...

In C, the order of bytes in an *int* are not defined. This program overwrote the $0xEF$ with $0x22$ on a Mac, but there are other platforms where it would overwrite the $0xDE$ instead - because the order of the bytes that make up the *int* were reversed. Therefore, when writing a program, you should never rely on the behavior of overwriting specific data in a union because it's not portable.

For more reading on the ordering of bytes, check out *endianness*.

Chapter 4

Making Decisions

Expect problems and eat them for breakfast.

Alfred A. Montapert

4.1 *if* / *else* Conditional Statement

Without conditional statements our code would be very boring. The code would follow the same path every time. A sequential fixed flow. They allow us to choose from different 'options'. Operations can happen under 'certain' conditions.

An example of a conditional statement, would be if you press a certain key on the keyboard, you would perform some operation, such as add a character to a string array.

An uncomplicated example of the 'if/else' statement is:

```
1  void main()
2  {
3      int a = 1;
4      if ( a > 0 ) // Conditional statement
5      {
6          printf("a is greater than 0");
7      }
```

```
 8      else
 9      {
10          printf("a not greater 0");
11      }
12  }
```

4.2 *switch / case*

For multiple choices based on a single condition it's tidier and more flexible to use the switch/case statement.

For example:

```
 1  void main()
 2  {
 3    int a = 2;
 4
 5    switch ( a ) // choice
 6    {
 7      case 0: // if a == 0
 8      {
 9        printf("a==0");
10      }
11      break;  // Warning! don't forget the break;!!  Otherwise, it ←
              will fall through to the next case, in this case, the case a←
              ==1.
12
13      case 1: // if a == 1
14      {
15        printf("a==1");
16      }
17      break;
18
19      case 2: // if a == 2
20      {
21        printf("a==1");
22      }
23      break;
24
25      default: // default - everything else, e.g., if a==20
26      {
27        printf("default - everything else");
28      }
29      break;
30    } // End of the swtich statement
31  }
```

4.3 Don't Confuse Operators = And ==

Novice programmers often stumble upon this simple problem. Even when you are in a rush typing and accidentally type '=' instead of '==' your program can compile without errors or warnings. Remember, the assignment operator '=' is for setting value, while the equality operator '==' is for comparing (i.e., true or false).

For example:

```
1  void main()
2  {
3     int a = 4;
4
5     if ( a=2 ) // ** Notice the serious issue??
6     {
7       print("a is 4\n");
8     }
9  }
```

The program will output 'a is 4'. Why? Because the operation within the if statement will perform the operation (i.e., assign 2 to 'a'), then any number other than zero is counted as true in C++, so the code will execute the print statement.

How can we avoid this? Well try and avoid doing operating on a single line (i.e., within the conditional statement). Also, when doing comparisons, try and perform good practices, and put the constant number on the left, i.e., 2==a. If you type, 2=a, you'll get a compiler error.

4.4 Order Of Operations Matters (e.g., Multiplication, Assignment, and Addition)

The operations follow the same priority as standard mathematics, for example, multiplication and division taking priority over addition and subtraction.

```
1  void main()
2  {
3     int a = 2 * 3 + 4 % 2 - 5;
4     printf("a = %d\n");
5  }
```

4.5 Loops (*while, do − while, for*)

Repeating specific sections of code using the three conditional statements (i.e., while, do-while, and for).

```
1  void main()
2  {
3     //-------------------while loop -------------
```

```
 4    int a = 0;
 5    while ( a < 10 )
 6    {
 7      printf("a: %d\n");
 8      a++;
 9    }//End while(..)
10  }
```

```
 1  void main()
 2  {
 3    //-------------------do-while loop-----------
 4    int a = 0;
 5    do
 6    {
 7      printf("a: %d\n");
 8      a++;
 9    }
10    while ( a < 10 );
11  }
```

```
 1  void main()
 2  {
 3    //-----------------for loop-----------
 4    for (int a=0; a<10; ++a)
 5    {
 6      printf("a: %d\n");
 7    }
 8  }
```

4.6 Infinite Loops

A loop becomes infinite an loop, if a condition never becomes false. The 'while' loop is a good example for this purpose. Since the expressions that forms the 'while' loop can be set to true (or 1). Creating an endless loop by leaving the conditional expression always the same. There are several possibilities to do an infinite loop (endless loop), here are a few you would choose:

```
 1  for(;;) {}
 2  while(1) {} / while(true) {}
 3  do {} while(1) / do {} while(true)
```

Infinite loops can also arise as bugs.

```
 1  void main()
 2  {
 3    // This code will loop forever, since 'a' is a char
 4    // variable, which has a range from 0 to 256
 5
 6    char a = 0;
 7    while ( a < 1024 ) // loop forever!
```

```
 8     {
 9        a++;
10     }
11  }
```

An example of where you might come across an infinite loop in a computer game might be the update loop - which encapsulate the entire logic/update/render and is called each frame until the game is over.

4.7 'Break'ing The Loop

The keyword 'break' can be inserted inside any loop to exit the loop early. The 'break' statement will only break out of the current loop. Hence, if you're in nested loops, the break condition will only exit you from the loop you're executing within.

```
 1  void main()
 2  {
 3     int a = 0;
 4     while ( true )
 5     {
 6        printf("a: %d\n", a);
 7
 8        a++;
 9
10        if ( a > 5 )
11        {
12           break; // when this line of code is executed
13        }          //           |
14     } // End while   |
15     //<----------------+
16  }
```

4.8 Nesting

We can nest loops and if statements within other loops and if statements.

```
 1  void main()
 2  {
 3     for (int i=0; i<10; ++i)
 4     {
 5        for (int k=0; k<20; ++k)
 6        {
 7           printf("i: %d, k: %d\n", i, k);
 8
 9        }// End for( k..)
10     }// End for( i.. )
11  }
```

Chapter 5

Functions

A black cat or a white cat, is a good cat, so long as it catches the mice.

A Chinese Proverb

A functions allow us to structure a program into segments of code that perform individual tasks. This is ideal if we have large program. As we can break the problem up into smaller tasks. Similarly, if a task needs executing multiple times, we can just call the function multiple times without duplicating code. Each time a task finishes executing the function returns to the place in code it was called from. In fact, we have already been using a function from the start, the 'program entry point' **main()** is a function in itself.

```
1   void main()
2   {
3
4   }// End main()
```

The crucial things to remember about a function is: a function relates an input to an output (analogous to a machine that has an input and an output). We pass parameters to function through internal registers or memory (e.g., the stack or heap which we get to later). The function performs its operation, for example, printing text on the screen or asking if a key has been pressed. Then returns to the place in code that called it.

The crucial elements of a function are:

1. each function has a unique name (e.g., print),
2. each function has a return type (e.g., default may be void),
3. each function takes parameters (e.g., default may be void),
4. when a function reaches the end of its block of code, it returns to the place it was called from.

5.1 Function Syntax

```
/*
 +--- Return type
 |          +---- Function name
 |          |        +-- Open/Close parenthesis --+
 |          |        |      +-- Passed paramaters  |
 |          |        |      |                       |
\|/      \|/     \|/    \|/    \|/                   |
 |          |        |      |      |                 | */
int DoSomething( int a, char b ) // <-------+
{
  printf("DoSomething Function\");
  // Print out the passed arguments
  printf("a: %d, b: %c\n");
}
```

5.2 Declaring and Defining a function (.h/.cpp)

```
//------------------code.h-------------

void main();
int  dosomething(int a);
void cat();

//------------------code.cpp----------

void main()
{
  printf("main\n");
  dosomething(0); // call the dosomething function
}// End main(..)

int  dosomething(int a)
{
  printf("dosomething\n");
  cat(); // call the cat function
}// End dosomething(..)

void cat()
{
  printf("cat\n");
}//End cat(..)
```

5.3 Calling A Function

A function has a name and an optional set of parameters. While you can pass a number of parameters to the function you can only return one parameter. For example, the function 'main' is the compiled programs entry point.

```
int DoSomething( int arg0, char arg1, double arg2 )
{
    // Print the function name and the passed
    // arguments
    printf("DoSomething: %d, %c, %f\n", arg0, arg1 arg2);
    return 0; // return 0
}
```

5.4 Recursion

Functions can call themselves as is known as recursion. A recursive implementation can be an alternative approach to using loops. In some cases recursion can be more elegant an efficient.

For example, calculating the factorial number (i.e., 0!=1, 1!=1, 2!=3, 3!=6 ...)

```
int Factorial(int i)
{
    if ( 0==i )
    {
        return 1;
    }
    return i + Factorial( i-1 )
}// End Factorial(..)

// Program entry point
void main()
{
    // Print the factorial numbers from 0 to 6
    for (int i=0; i<6; ++i)
    {
        int factNum = Factorial(i);
        printf("0! = %d\n", factNum);
    }// End for
}// End main(..)
```

5.5 Overloading Functions

Functions can have the same 'name' but different arguments. For two functions with the same name the 'passed arguments' need to be different. If only the return argument is different it won't compile.

```
1   // Four different functions with the same name
2   int DoSomething(int a);                 //<--+
3   int DoSomething(int a, char c);         //   |
4   int DoSomething(int a, double b);       //<--|-+
5   int DoSomething();                      //<--|-|-+
6                                           //   | | |
7   void main()                             //   | | |
8   {                                       //   | | |
9     DoSomething(2);                       //---+ | |
10    DoSomething(34, 2.0);                 //-----+ |
11    DoSomething();                        //-------+
12  }
```

The compiler knows which function to call based on the arguments you pass to the function you are calling.

5.6 Default Arguments

Starting from the 'last' function argument you can set the variables default values. Note, you have to set all the arguments to the right. Default arguments is useful feature that enables you to show the developer what typical values would be used.

```
1   void MyFunction(int a, int b=2, int c=9)
2   {
3     printf("MyFunction a:%d, b:%d, c:%c\n");
4   }
5
6   void main()
7   {
8     // Call the function and leave default
9     // arguments alone
10    MyFunction(1);        // b and c default
11    MyFunction(2,5);      // overload b with 5
12    MyFunction(5,9,12);   // overload b and c
13  }
```

5.7 Variable Scope

The 'curly' brackets dictate the scope. Variables can have the same name within different curly brackets. To choose a variable from another scope you use the "::" operator.

```
1   int a = 22; // global variable
2   void main()
3   {
4     int a = 5;// local variable
5     printf("a = %d\n", a);     // print local variable
```

```
6     printf("a = %d\n", ::a); // print global variable
7   }
```

```
1   void main()
2   {
3     int b = 2;
4     {
5       int b = 33;
6       int c = 44;
7
8       printf("b = %d\n", b);    // print local 'b'
9       printf("b = %d\n", ::b); // print outer scope 'b'
10    }
11    // You can't access variable 'c' here as it's
12    // gone out of scope
13  }
```

5.8 Static Functions And Static Variables

A static function can only be called within the specific 'cpp' file. This can be useful if you want a particular function to only be used by the functions within that file, for example, a helper function.

A static variable is analogous to a global variable, however, it can only be accessed within the function. The static variable will be initialized the first time the function is called and will keep the values.

```
1   void Count()
2   {
3     static int s = 0; // This line will only done once
4     s++;
5     printf("s: %d\n", s);
6   }//End Count(..)
7
8   void main()
9   {
10    Count(); // Will print 1
11    Count(); // Will print 2
12    Count(); // Will print 3
13    ...
14  }//End main(..)
```

Chapter 6

Nuts & Bolts of Object Oriented Programming

You are never too old to set another goal or to dream a new dream.

C. S. Lewis

6.1 C++, Extensions to C

The largest extension from C to C++ is classes. Classes are a way of wrapping data and functions together. Classes allow us to decide access levels for variables and functions, such as private or public.

Similar to how we can instant a variable we can also instant a whole class. Classes enable us to write code that is more readable.

6.2 Why Object Oriented Programming (OOP)?

The reason we prefer to use object orientated programming languages like C++ is it provides:

- More readable code
- Code that is less error prone
- Encapsulate data and functions

6.2.1 Data Abstraction (Black-Box)

Writing empty abstract classes that form a type of map. Hiding the implementation details. Abstraction means providing only essential information to the outside world and hiding the background details. For example, when you use your computer, you can see the monitor, keyboard, and mouse. You don't know anything about the internal wiring or circuitry - this is abstraction.

So in software, if you're designing a program to deal with inventory, and you'd like to be able to find out how many items of a certain type the system has in stock. From the perspective of the interface system, you don't if you're getting this information from a database, a text file, a remote repository interface or punch cards. You just care that you can say "myitem.GetItemsInStock();" and know that it will return an integer.

If you later decide that you want to record that number in some other way, the person designing the interface doesn't need to know, care or worry about it as long as myitem accessor still has the GetItemsInStock() method. Like wise, the interface doesn't need to care if you add additional accessors, such as, 'GetSquareRootOfItems()' method. You can pass an instance of the new class to it just as well.

Hence, you've hidden the details of how the data is acquired and decided that anything with a GetItemsInStock() method is an instance of the same class (or a subclass thereof) for certain purposes.

6.2.2 Encapsulation

Encapsulation is the packing of data and functions into a single component. The features of encapsulation are supported using classes in most object-oriented programming languages, although other alternatives also exist. It allows selective hiding of properties and methods in an object by building an impenetrable wall to protect the code from accidental corruption.

6.2.3 Polymorphism

If you think about the Greek roots of the term, it should become obvious.

Poly = many: polygon = many-sided, polystyrene = many styrenes (a), polyglot = many languages, and so on. Morph = change or form: morphology

= study of biological form, Morpheus = the Greek god of dreams able to take any form.

Polymorphism is a long word for a very simple concept.

Polymorphism describes a pattern in object oriented programming in which classes have different functionality while sharing a common interface.

The beauty of polymorphism is that the code working with the different classes does not need to know which class it is using since theyre all used the same way. A real world analogy for polymorphism is a button. Everyone knows how to use a button: you simply apply pressure to it. What a button does, however, depends on what it is connected to and the context in which it is used but the result does not affect how it is used. If your boss tells you to press a button, you already have all the information needed to perform the task.

In the programming world, polymorphism is used to make applications more modular and extensible. Instead of messy conditional statements describing different courses of action, you create interchangeable objects that you select based on your needs. That is the basic goal of polymorphism.

6.3 The Laws of Inheritances

The product of inheritance is a classification Hierarchy. This is a relationship between classes where one class is said to be 'a kind of' other class. As the class hierarchy is traversed from top to bottom, we move from generalisation to specialisation of classes. This is done by adding functionality to extend what exists at each level of the class hierarchy from the base class. **Very important to remember, the order of constructor calls is 'top down' and follows the inheritance graph.** Don't get it confused. Also the keyword 'virtual' but we'll get to that in a moment.

6.4 What is a class?

The main purpose of C++ programming is to add object orientation to the C programming language and classes are the central feature of C++ that supports object-oriented programming and are often called user-defined types.

A class is used to specify the form of an object and it combines data representation and methods for manipulating that data into one neat package. The data and functions within a class are called members of the class.

6.5 Declaring A Class

When you define a class, you define a blueprint for a data type. This doesn't actually define any data, but it does define what the class name means, that is, what an object of the class will consist of and what operations can be performed on such an object.

```
1  class AClass
2  {
3    public int m_int;   // member variable called m_int;
4  }; //<-- **** Very important *** Don't forget to put
5     /       a 'semi-colon' at the end of the class defition
```

6.6 Don't Forget The ";" At The End

If you forget the semi-colon at the end of the class declaration it will cause a number of errors. In large files the error can be shown in the .cpp file and not the .h file where the missing semi-colon are located.

6.7 Access Specifiers (Public/Protected/Private)

```
1  class AClass // class name
2  {
3    public:     m_a;
4    private:    m_b;
5    protected:  m_c;
6  }; // <--- don't forget the semi-colon
```

6.8 Constructors/Destructors

The constructor and destructor have the same name as the class. The constructor and destructor are called automatically when the class is created and destroyed.

```
1  class AClass
2  {
3    AClass() // Constructor
4    {
5      printf("Constructor\n");
6    }//End AClass
7    ~AClass() // Destructor
```

```
 8    {
 9       printf("Destructor\n");
10    }//End ~AClass
11  }; // End class AClass
```

6.9 Static Members

Static member variables must be initialized when they are declared in a class;

```
 1  class AClass
 2  {
 3    static int m_var = 0; // 'static' must be initialized
 4
 5    static void DoFunc() // 'static'
 6    {
 7      m_var = 1;
 8    }// End DoFunc()
 9
10  }; // End class AClass
```

6.10 friends

In principle, private and protected members of a class cannot be accessed from outside the same class in which they are declared. However, this rule does not apply to "friends".

Friends are functions or classes declared with the friend keyword.

6.11 Inheritance

Classes in C++ can be extended, creating new classes which retain characteristics of the base class. This process, known as inheritance, involves a base class and a derived class: The derived class inherits the members of the base class, on top of which it can add its own members.

For example, let's imagine a series of classes to describe two kinds of polygons: rectangles and triangles. These two polygons have certain common properties, such as the values needed to calculate their areas: they both can be described simply with a height and a width (or base).

6.12 Overriding

If you derive a class from a base class with member functions of the same name and arguments (note, both name and arguments, not just one or the other!). If you create an instance of the derived class and access the member function with the duplicate name, "only" the member function in derived class is invoked (i.e., the member function of derived class overrides the member function of base class). This feature in C++ programming is known as function overriding.

```
class A
{
    .... ... ....
    public:
      void get_data()
      {
          .... ... ....
      }
};

class B : public A
{
    .... ... ....
    public:
      void get_data()
      {
          .... ... ....
      }
};

int main()
{
    B obj;
    .... ... ....
    obj.get_data();
}
```


Figure 6.1. *Overriding Member Functions* - *Inhereted class member functions can have the same name. Which one gets called?*

6.13 'pure' virtual

What is the purpose of a virtual function? What happens when we doing use the key term 'virtual' with a methods declaration? A virtual function means that it can be replaced with a function of the same name and parameters by an inherited class. If you inherit from a class and don't put the virtual keyword then the wrong function will be called.

```
1  class base
2  {
3    void funcA()  // *** NOTE 'no' virtual keyword
4    {
5      printf("base:funcA()\n");
6    }// End funcA()
7
8    virtual void funcB() //** NOTE 'virtual'..
9    {
10     printf("base:funcB()\n");
11   }// End funcA()
12 }; //<-- don't forget semi-colon
13
14 class childA
15 {
16   void funcA()
17   {
18     printf("childA:funcA()\n");
19   }// End funcA()
20
21   void funcB()
22   {
23     printf("childA:funcB()\n");
24   }// End funcB()
25 }; //<-- don't forget semi-colon
26
27 class childB
28 {
29   void funcA()
30   {
31     printf("childB:funcA()\n");
32   }// End funcA()
33
34   void funcB()
35   {
36     printf("childB:funcB()\n");
37   }// End funcB()
38 }; //<-- don't forget semi-colon
39
40 // Program Entry Point
41 void main()
42 {
43   // Test out our class 'virtual' functions
44   //**1** Start simple, test
45   base* cA = new childA();
46   base* cB = new childB();
47
48   cA->funcA(); // prints 'base'
49   cB->funcA(); // prints 'childB'
50
51   cA->funcB(); // prints 'base'
52   cB->funcB(); // prints 'childB'
53
54   // Always for every 'new' you 'delete' or you'll
55   // leak memory!!
56   delete cA;
57   delete cB;
58 }// End main(..)
```

If you don't include the keyword 'virtual' the base class is always called and
'NOT' the inherited class function as we want.

Do I need to put the keyword 'virtual' everywhere? In short, you only need to put it in the base class. However, programmers commonly put it in inherited classes to help developers see at first glance that the function is virtual.

6.14 Copy-Constructor

A function with the same name as the class is a constructor. However, when we use the equality sign (i.e., '=') the copy constructor is called. We are creating a copy of the class and not a new instance.

If you aren't using a copy-constructor - override it and put an assert in it! A copy constructor can be extremely problematic if copies of classes are being made with pointers to memory allocated (e.g., new and delete).

```cpp
1   // A problematic example of not overriding the copy-constructor
2   // and leaving the default copy-constructor to do the work
3   class ClassA
4   {
5   public:
6     // Each class has a memory pointer
7     char* m_ptr;
8
9     ClassA() // Constructor
10    {
11      m_ptr = new char[10];
12    }// End ClassA()
13
14    ~ClassA() // Destructor
15    {
16      delete [] m_ptr;    // Warning****, notice we are using
17                          // 'delete []' with square brackets
18                          // since it's an array - if you don't
19                          // use the square brackets, and do
20                          // 'delete m_ptr', it will only delete
21                          // the first item in the array and lead
22                          // to a memory leak
23    } // End ~ClassA()
24
25  }; //End ClassA
26
27  // Program entry point
28  void main()
29  {
30     ClassA a;
31     ClassA b = a; // default copy-constructor
32     // The copy-constructor will replace the pointer of m_ptr in 'b'
33     // with the m_ptr from 'a' without freeing it first or copying
34     // the individual elements.
35     // Hence when both 'a' and 'b' are destroyed, they will both
36     // try and delete the same pointer!!  Memory assert!
37     // Also if instance 'a' changes the memory, it will be changed
38     // in instance 'b' - they won't have unique copies.
39  }
```

6.15 Managers - Creating/Destroying/Managing Classes

Rather than having classes or structures created or destroyed at any place in the code (e.g., new'ing or deleting instances, such as ClassA* a = new classA(); We can make the constructor private (or protected). Hence, the we are unable to create an instance of the class. So how do we create an instance then? The solution is to add a static manager function to the class. The creation and destruction of instances must go through the static manager functions. This allows us to keep track of the creation or destruction of class objects.

This can be useful if we want to keep track of objects being allocated or created. For example, if we want to keep a list of objects, and rather than destroying and re-creating instances, they are activated and de-activated from a pool. Since in practice, allocating and deallocating large numbers of objects can be computationally expensive and result in memory fragmentation.

```
class ClassP
{
// Note the constructor is 'private' - so you can't create
// an instance of the class - only by calling Create()
private:
   ClassP() // Constructor
   {
   }// End ClassP()

public:
   static ClassP* Create()
   {
      return new ClassP();
   }// End Create()

   static void Destroy(ClassP* p)
   {
      delete p;
   }// End Destroy(..)
}; // End ClassP

// Program entry point
void main()
{
   ClassP* p = ClassP::Create();

   // Make sure we releate, so we don't get memory leaks
   ClassP::Detroy(p);
}// End main()
```

6.15.1 Singleton

Without making all the member functions and member variables static, we
can write the class so that a only a single instance of the class always exists.

```
1  class ClassS
2  {
3  public:
4     ClassS* GetInstance()
5     {
6     }// End GetInstance()
7
8  }; // End ClassS
```

6.16 operator overloading +/=*

Operator overloading is just so useful. It makes the code cleaner, more
concise, and readable. Object orientated languages, such as Java, possess
many of the high level features of C++. However, Java doesn't have operator
overloading. So why is operator overloading so great? It allows us to perform
operations intuitively, for example, if we have two vector objects we can add
then using the '+' operator, and subtract them with the '-' operator, instead
of using 'add' and 'subtract' functions.

6.16.1 e.g. Vector, Matrix

```
1   // Basic vector3 class
2   class Vector3
3   {
4      public x, y, z;
5   }; // End Vector3 class
6
7   // Global operator
8   Vector3 operator+ (const Vector3& lhs, const Vector3& rhs)
9   {
10     Vector3 res;
11     res.x = lhs.x + rhs.x;
12     res.y = lhs.y + rhs.y;
13     res.z = lhs.z + rhs.z;
14     return res;
15  }// End operator+
16
17  // Program entry point
18  void main()
19  {
20     Vector3 a;
21     a.x=1;
22     a.y=2;
23     a.z=3;
24     Vector3 b = a;
25     Vector3 c = a + b; // Operator overloading!!!
```

26   `}// End main()`

6.16.2 Java Can't Do This

For whatever reason, it was decided during the development of Java that it would not support operator overloading. Since Java is a managed language, it might have seemed that operator overloading would be a performance hit or wouldn't be worth the extra effort.

Chapter 7

Understanding Memory

By failing to prepare, you are preparing to fail.

Benjamin Franklin

7.1 Why do we need to understand memory?

Memory is a limited resource. There are various memory types. C++ gives direct access to the system resources for maximum speed and control. Whether you want to write a highly optimized animation system or a real-time rasterization renderer. You can do this in C++.

7.2 What is a pointer? (*)

A pointer is analogous to an address. A pointer is basically a number. You store data in memory. The location in memory of that data (i.e., the address) is stored as a pointer. You declare a pointer the same way you declare a variable with the exception of 'asterix'. For example, if you have an character (i.e., char) in memory and you want a pointer to it.

7.2.1 How can I get a variables address? (i.e., ampersand)

You can obtain the address of a variables location in memory by using the 'ampersand'. Note, if the variable is created by allocating the memory on the 'heap' (i.e., with new or malloc system functions), you'll be given the pointer to the memory.

For example:

```
1  // First create a character variable called 'c' and
2  // put the letter 't' in it
3  char c = 't';
4  // Now create a pointer and point it at our character
5  char* p = &c;
```

7.3 Indirect Operators

You may ask, if you have a pointer, how do you access or modify the data the pointer points to? There are two common ways, they are:

- 'asterix' operator (e.g., char* p = &c; *p = 'n')
- array accessor (e.g., char* p = &c; p[0] = 'n;)

7.4 Using pointers to objects $(->)$

For pointers to objects (i.e., classes or structure), you can access member functions and variables using the 'arrow' operator (i.e., $->$).

For example:

```
1   // Very basic class with some public variables
2   // and func
3   class SomeClass
4   {
5   public:
6      int a;
7      int b;
8      void fun()
9      {
10        printf("called fun\n");
11     }// End fun()
12  };
13
14  // Demonstrate the 'arrow' accessor operator
15  // Program entry point
16  void main()
17  {
18     // Traditionally
```

```
19    SomeClass someA;
20    someA.a = 2;
21    someA.fun();
22
23    // Using pointers and the indirect operator
24    SomeClass* someB = new SomeClass();
25    someB->b = 33;
26    someB->fun();    // Notice we use '->' instead of '.'
27    delete someB;    // Release memory (we don't want leaks)
28  }// End main
```

A side note, we can 'cast' the pointer to an instance using a '*' and access the class variables using the dot operator.

For example:

```
1  SomeClass* someC = new SomeClass();
2  (*someC).a = 88;
3  (*someC).fun();
```

As you become familiar with casing between pointers, addresses, and instances, you'll learn all sorts of tricks and approaches, some more elegant than others.

```
1   // Get address using '&' and use the address like a pointer
2   SomeClass someD;
3   (&someD)->a = 3;
4
5   // Bit different, but store address in an integeger variable,
6   // and later cast it back to the class type and use it.
7   SomeClass* someE = new SomeClass();
8   int add = (int)someE;
9   ((SomeClass*)add)->fun()
10  delete someE;
```

7.5 Allocating and de-allocating memory

Well this isn't really 'new', since you've been doing this previously, to demonstrate pointers. The main way of allocating and deallocating memory in C++ is with 'new' and 'delete'. With the older C language, you would use 'malloc' and 'free'

1st allocating single instances

```
1  int* p = new int;    // allocate a 'single' integer pointer
2                       // variable is called 'p'
3  delete p;            // release the memory
4  p = NULL;            // good habbit - null the pointer
```

2nd allocating arrays

```
1  int* pa = new int[100]; // allocate an 'array' of 100 integers
2                  // variable is called 'pa'
3  delete[] pa;        // release the 'block' of memory
4                  // **warning** if you don't do the brackets '[]'
5                  // you will only release first element and cause
6                  // a memory leak
7  pa = NULL;          // good habbit - the memory is gone - null it
```

Just be careful if you allocate an array that you delete an array and not a single instance. Furthermore, attempting to use released memory. That is why we null the pointer, so it's easier to identify if the memory has been deleted. It can be very difficult tracking down errors due to invalid memory calls since the memory address can look valid but have been deleted by the system.

7.5.1 Heap or Stack?

So why do we bother with the heap or stack? Why don't we just do everything on the stack? In a nutshell, you only have a limited amount of stack when the program starts up. Each time functions and variables are used they are pushed and popped on the stack without your control. However, the heap is larger and gives you greater control (i.e., dynamic control) over what is created and destroyed at any time.

7.6 What is in the memory? Random!

Memory is a finite resource. It's typically large enough for you not to worry about (i.e., many megabytes). The memory is organized into different types. Such as data and execution code and the hardware keeps track of this. When you run your program it's loaded into memory and the processor starts execution from the program entry point (i.e., main).

In time, you'll get a feel for what the different memory values mean and what are good, bad, and corrupted values. For example:

- 0xABABABAB : Used by Microsoft's HeapAlloc() to mark "no man's land" guard bytes after allocated heap memory
- 0xABADCAFE : A startup to this value to initialize all free memory to catch errant pointers
- 0xBAADF00D : Used by Microsoft's LocalAlloc(LMEMFIXED) to mark uninitialised allocated heap memory
- 0xBADCAB1E : Error Code returned to the Microsoft's VC debugger when connection is severed to the debugger

- 0xBEEFCACE : Used by Microsoft .NET as a magic number in resource files
- 0xCCCCCCCC : Used by Microsoft's C++ debugging runtime library to mark uninitialised stack memory
- 0xCDCDCDCD : Used by Microsoft's C++ debugging runtime library to mark uninitialised heap memory
- 0xDEADDEAD : A Microsoft Windows STOP Error code used when the user manually initiates the crash.
- 0xFDFDFDFD : Used by Microsoft's C++ debugging heap to mark "no man's land" guard bytes before and after allocated heap memory
- 0xFEEEFEEE : Used by Microsoft's HeapFree() to mark freed heap memory

7.6.1 Custom Memory Manager

Allocating and deallocating memory can be a performance hit. Especially when you are allocating and deallocating hundreds or thousands of times per frame. Typically, you'll avoid allocating and deallocating memory during your game and use memory pools. Furthermore, it's common for your game to grab all the available memory at startup, and manage it yourself. You keep track of fragmentation and which game resources are using memory and how much (e.g., animation gets x amount of memory, terrain x amount, physics x amount and so on). You can overload any of the memory allocation functions or operators and integrate in your own memory manager without too much damage to your code.

7.7 Leaking Memory (a sinking ship)

Even a small leak will eventually cause your program to come crashing down. When you allocate memory, you are making a contract with the system that the allocated memory should be available and you need it. While you might think with today's high end computers that memory is huge - it's still finite. Keep track of allocated and de-allocated memory. If you do have a leak it should be easy to identify and track down if you have wrapped the memory allocation operators. You don't want to be running your game and find that after 5 or 10 minutes it starts to slow down. Then after 20 minutes your system crashes to a halt.

7.8 Constants (Const), Safety, and Reliability

The 'const' operator is there to help you. The 'const' operator is so the compiler can alert you to any errors or issues that might have happened in the code during compile time. It also allows the compiler to make some assumptions and optimize the code appropriately. However, be warned, the 'const' is just a syntax checker. You can still bypass the 'const' and cast the const variable to a non-const.

For example:

```
1  const int a = 4;
2  a = 5; // *ERROR* won't compile
3
4  (int)a = 5;   // allowed but you shouldn't really change a const
5
6  // You can also use 'const_cast'
7  const int j = 3;       // j is declared const
8  int*    pj = const_cast<int*>(&j);
9  *pj        = 4;        // allowed but can cause undefined behavior :-/
```

7.9 Arrays

An array is a 'block' of memory. An array can be of any type. We can allocate an array of 'raw' memory and cast it to a specific type (e.g., int, byte, float, class or structure). The majority of time you are working large chunks of data so it's easier to work with chunks of memory and iterate over them (i.e, arrays of data).

7.9.1 Dynamic Arrays

While you can allocate arrays on the 'stack', it's more efficient and controllable if you allocate memory on 'heap'.

```
1  void main()
2  {
3    // Scope operator
4    { // Comes in here and array is allocated
5      int a[100];
6    } // array 'a' is destroyed
7
8    int* b = new int[222]; // allocate int array of 222
9    delete[] b;           // delete memory
10   b = NULL;
11
12 }// End main()
```

7.9.2 Character Arrays (Strings)

Character arrays are special, since a character array is a 'string'. We are constantly typing and manipulating strings. A string is just an array of 'char' variables. If you have used high level languages such as 'Java' and 'Python' you might find string operations a little more challenging. Since you have to actually do the work yourself, that is, go character by character and perform the operation. Furthermore, you have to be aware of 'low' level string principles. Such as strings always have a 'null' terminating character at the end, new-lines are identified by the special character '
n'.

```
1  #include <stdio.h> // printf(..)
2  void main()
3  {
4    // Create a string of characters
5    char str[] = "Once upon a time";
6    // Length of str is 16 + 1
7    // The '+1' is a 'null' character indicating the
8    // end of a string.
9    printf("str: %s", str);
10 }// End main()
```

I've focused on 'ascii' strings. Each character is 'one' byte each. However, there is also unicode with each character being represented by a wchar (i.e., 2 or more bytes) for complex languages such as Russian and Chinese. Nevertheless, the same principles apply, you just have a different set of characters.

7.10 String Manipulation

We should show some basic string manipulation tasks. For example, converting all the characters in a string to 'uppercase'.

```
1  #include <stdio.h>  // printf(..)
2  #include <string>   // toupper(..)
3  void main()
4  {
5    char str[] = "once, not twice, but once a long time ago";
6    printf("str: %s#n", str); // print str now
7
8    // convert all the characters to upper case
9
10   // 1st, lets see how many characters we have
11   // This should be 45 using the string above
12   int len = strlen(str);
13
14   // 2nd loop over each character and make it uppercase
15   for (int i=0; i<len; ++i)
16   {
17     str[i] = toupper( str[i] );
```

```
18    }// End for
19
20    printf("str: %s#n", str); // print 'uppercase' version of str
21
22  } // End main()
```

7.11 Converting Numbers To Strings And Back

You can't just 'cast' a string to a integer. For example:

```
1  char str[] = "223";
2  int val = (int)str;   // wrong wrong wrong
```

If you do this, you'll not get the value '223' but instead you'll get the memory address for the pointer (e.g., something like 0xF036E723).

Two useful functions part of the standard C libraries are 'atoi' and 'itoa' for converting between numbers and ascii.

```
1  #include <stdio.h> // atoi, itoa
2  // Program entry point
3  void main()
4  {
5    // string to integer
6    char str0[] = "123";
7    int val0   = atoi(str);
8
9    // integer to string - itoa is a bit more complex as you have to
10   // specify the base (i.e., hex, decimal, oct)
11   int val1 = 98;
12   char str1[22];   // Allocate a array of characters for the string
13   // Definition:
14   // char *  itoa ( int value, char * str, int base );
15   itoi( val1, str1, 10 );
16
17   // Print out our strings and numbers, so we
18   // know it worked
19   printf("str0: %s,  val0: %d"\n, str0, val0 );
20   printf("str1: %s,  val1: %d"\n, str1, val1 );
21
22  }// End main()
```

You can also use 'spring' for converting numbers to string. 'sprintf' also allows you to formulate complex strings that are a mix of different types (e.g., floats, substrings, and integers).

7.12 Passing And Returning 'Reference (&)', 'Pointer (*)' or 'Value'

```
1  void funcR(int& A);  // by reference
2  void funcP(int* A);  // by pointer
3  void funcV(int  A);  // by value
```

7.13 Endianness

Big-Endian & Little-Endian The terms endian and endianness refer to the convention used to interpret the bytes making up a data word when those bytes are stored in computer memory. In computing, memory commonly stores binary data by organizing it into 8-bit units called bytes. When reading or writing a data word consisting of multiple such units, the order of the bytes stored in memory determines the interpretation of the data word.

- little endian CPUs - x86, i7, intel/amd processors
- big endian CPUs - Power PC, Xbox360, PS3

While you may think the majority of processors are little endian, due to windows and the intel/amd processor, however, there are still plenty of servers using Sun's UltraSparc CPUs, that are generally big endian, though the latest models can be either big or little endian. There are many CPUs that can be either one or the other (e.g. ARM, still used in many devices like mobile phones and the like), as supporting both adds greatest flexibility for the hardware and for the software vendors. Even the IA64 CPUs (the Intanium, that was intended to replace x86 before AMD invented x86-64, that was true 64 bit and could only emulate 32 bit, unlike x86-64 that can be both) is one of the CPUs that can be switched to big endian. CPUs that can be both are called bi-endian.

Actually if we ignore Intel (and compatible CPUs) for a second, most CPUs on the market are either big endian or at least bi-endian, though most of these are not used in any consumer PCs as far as I know.

However, we can easily resolve any endian issues with a few extra lines of code. While modern CPU can swap endian in hardware. Alternatively, we can write a program on a little endian Intel CPU, that swaps endianess of every integer read from memory and again when writing back to memory, this will cause maybe a performance penalty as little as 5%; and in practice we'll only need to swap endianess for data coming in and going out of our application, as within our application the endianess is constant, of course.

Also note: most network protocols specify byte order to be big endian, TCP/IP being the most familiar family. So if we work on lower network layers, we will always have to continue swapping bytes

```
1   #define ByteSwap16(n) \
2   (((((unsigned int) n) << 8) & 0xFF00) | \
3   (((( unsigned int) n) >> 8) & 0x00FF) )
4
5   #define ByteSwap32(n) \
6   (((((unsigned long) n) << 24) & 0xFF000000) |    \
7   ((( (unsigned long) n) <<  8) & 0x00FF0000) |    \
8   ((( (unsigned long) n) >>  8) & 0x0000FF00) |    \
9   ((( (unsigned long) n) >> 24) & 0x000000FF) )
10
11  ///////////// Endian swaping wrapper functions //////////
12  inline void fwrite32(UInt32 blah, FILE *f)
13  {
14  UInt32 item = ByteSwap32(blah);
15  fwrite(&item, 4, 1, f);
16  }
17
18  inline void fwrite16(UInt16 blah, FILE *f)
19  {
20  UInt16 item = ByteSwap16(blah);
21  fwrite(&item, 2, 1, f);
22  }
```

Listing 7.1. Endian changing example for a 2 byte and 4 byte value.

Chapter 8

Templates

If you can dream it, you can do it.

Walt Disney

8.1 What Is A Template?

Template allow you to dynamically create different 'types' at compile time. For example, if you want to create a function that takes an 'int' or a 'float' Instead of writing two functions, you would write one function but specify the variable 'type' as a template. The compiler will automatically generate the two types at compile time for you.

8.2 Why Do We Need Templates?

Identical code that is only different based on type (i.e., variable type, such as integer or float) is error prone. Each time you fix a problem in one place you need to repeat the same multiple times. If you decide you need the code to work with a new type, the code has to be repeated. Hence, templates provide an elegant way of reducing the redundant repeating and automatically generate the solution.

```
1   // For example, we have two identical functions
2   // called double - however, one works with floats and
3   // the other with integers
4   int Double(int val)
5   {
6       return val * 2;
7   }// End Double
8
9   float Double(float val)
10  {
11    return val * 2;
12  }// End Double
13
14  void main()
15  {
16    Double( 2.0f );
17    Double( 2 );
18
19  }// End main()
```

8.3 Over Using Templates

On occasion people can go template 'happy'. Implementing everything in templates with the mindset that it's more flexible and expandable. However, templates are like any tool. They have a right place and a right time. Overusing them can make your code-base unreadable, bloated, and difficult to customize.

8.4 Template Example

```
1   template<class TYPE>   // 1 - we need to say we are using a template
2   TYPE Double(TYPE val) // 2 - we use TYPE instead of the variable ←
        type
3   {
4     return val * 2;
5   }// End Double
6
7   void main()
8   {
9     Double( 2.0f );
10    Double( 2 );
11
12  }// End main()
```

8.5 Template Functions, Classes, Parameters

The concept is relatively straightforward once you get into the habit of creating using templates. You first ensure you have 'template<class TYPE>'
at the start before the function or class, then you use the 'TYPE' declaration
for the dynamic type you want created at compile time.

8.5.1 Classes Need A Little Extra <>

Since you can create an instance of a class without passing any parameters,
how does the class know which instance type to create? Hence, when you
create a class instance, you need to add an additional explicit type in triangle
brackets so the compiler doesn't get confused.

```
1   template<class TYPE>
2   class Item
3   {
4       TYPE data;
5   public:
6       Item() { }
7
8       void SetData(TYPE nValue)
9       {
10          data = nValue;
11      }// End SetData(..)
12
13      TYPE GetData() const
14      {
15          return data;
16      }// End GetData()
17  };// End class Item
18
19  // Program Entry Point
20  void main()
21  {
22      // Instance of an integer class
23      Item<int>  a;
24      // Allocate pointer of float class
25      Item<float>* p = new Item<float>();
26  }// End main()
```

A note for when templates get so large that you need to use .h and .cpp files.
When you have a class implementation in the cpp file, you need to repeat
the template definition for each function.

```
1   // Temp.h
2   #ifndef TEMP_H
3   #define TEMP_H
4
5   template<class TYPE>
6   class Temp
7   {
8   public:
```

```
 9        Temp();
10        void SetValue(TYPE v);
11        TYPE Getalue();
12 private:
13        TYPE val;
14 };// End Temp class
15 #endif // TEMP_H
```

Listing 8.1. Simple template declaration example (Temp.h).

```
 1 // Temp.cpp
 2 #include "Temp.h"
 3
 4 template <class TYPE>
 5 Temp<T>::Temp()
 6 {
 7 }
 8
 9 template <class TYPE>
10 void Temp<TYPE>::SetValue( TYPE v )
11 {
12   val = v;
13 }// End SetValue(..)
14
15 template <class TYPE>
16 TYPE Temp<TYPE>::GetValue()
17 {
18     return val;
19 }// End GetValue()
```

Listing 8.2. Simple template definition example (Temp.cpp).

8.6 T or TYPE

You can use 'template<class TYPE>' or 'template<class T>'. It's simply a matter of preference.

8.7 Final Thoughts

Templates are valuable little tools. However, just don't overdo it. Don't write your whole system in templates. As over using templates makes the code inflexible and difficult to read.

Chapter 9

Errors and Exceptions

All our dreams can come true, if we have the courage to pursue them.

Walt Disney

9.1 Exceptions

When something goes wrong. For example, if we access invalid memory or do a divide-by-zero, what should the system do? Typically, the program will throw an exception. If you do not catch and deal with the exception, it will cause your program to terminate with an error. So how do we catch exceptions? How do we identify what and where the exception came from. What information is given with an exception? What are the advantages of exceptions for error control? We address these questions and more here in this section.

9.2 Exception Types

There are all sorts of types and flavours of exceptions. Typically, you will only come across a few in your daily programming duties. Some of the most common ones are:

- Divide-By-Zero - dividing any value by zero
- NaN's - when a calculation or operation results in a 'not-a-number'
- Rounding errors - when a floating point calculation exceeds the limits (or floating point calculation error)
- Out of memory

9.3 Try-Catch

So what code syntax do you use to catch these exceptions? The solution is 'try' and 'catch'.

```
1   // Program entry point
2   void main ()
3   {
4     try
5     {
6       throw 20;
7     }
8     catch (int e)
9     {
10      printf("An exception occurred. Exception Nr.\n");
11    }
12  }// End main()
```

9.4 Food For Thought

What you do when you detect an exception is upto you. For example, if an exception occurs after memory allocation, do you tidy up, release memory and try and recover, or just give a warning and close the program?

For example, upon catching an exception:

- nothing : You just continue and don't do anything - of course, this can cause leaks and breaking down of functionality just to die somewhere else
- minimum : You try and tidy up before continuing, i.e., if an exception is thrown you ensure no resources are leaked and all calculations and objects are still whole and correct but might be in a state that you don't desire
- maximum : You recover and repeat the task without any problems and the program continues on its merry way whole and happy (e.g., solving and recovering from any eventuality)

The try-catch method of debugging and catching errors is popular since it can avoid a multitude of nested flags and if/then statements across multiple functions. For example, if you detect an error, you can force throw an exception and have the code unwrap the call-stack cleanly and jump to the catch statement which can be nested within many sub function calls.

9.5 Don't Hide The Problem

Writing functions that 'recover' from a problem without informing you is bad! Of course, there is nothing wrong with having a function attempt to recover, however, you should trigger an assert or log the problem so that it can be fixed. For example, copying a string into a NULL memory location - instead of testing if the memory location is valid and returning, you should also assert to note that something might be wrong but you won't crash.

9.6 External Input

One of the largest cause of error is input from users or from external files. Never 'assume' anything when it comes to external influences. Use sanity checks to validate data and that values stay within pre-defined ranges. If the user needs to enter a digit in the range 0 to 100 - be sure to check the range (e.g., that we don't have strings, negative numbers, or values with decimal places).

Chapter 10

Practical Aspects

A person who never made a mistake never tried anything new.

Albert Einstein

10.1 Performance, Loops, and Delays

For interactive environments, such as games, we need to ensure that the frame-rate stays above a certain threshold (i.e., greater than real-time). Delays and performance hits can be caused by loading in assets, extreme computational calculations, or excessively nested loops.

Exploit multi-threading. For example, if you can send a task to another thread and leave it crunching away over multiple frames without it affecting the users experience, then why not? This might include, streaming assets in the background or updating the collision detection.

10.2 Robustness (i.e., Crashes)

Writing code that can stay afloat. No-one likes a game that just terminate. If anything, try and save the state and exit gracefully. Possibly, when the game reloads, it can continue where the player left off before the game so unfortunately crashed.

10.3 Release Builds

During the development of your game you will have different build versions. You will primarily add and test your early builds in debug. However, as the game moves closer to completion you will build release builds (i.e., optimized final versions with less debug code that might be causing slow-downs). Instead of debugging in the controlled development environment, you are left debugging using log files and information from testers who explain what they did to reach the problem.

10.4 Asserts

Asserts are great! They allow you to identify specific problems. For example, placing asserts at the beginning and end of functions allows you define a set of rules to ensure data going in and out is within specified tolerance. If values go out of range or are unexpected (e.g., passing a NAN to a function), you will get an informative assert. Of course in practice, you write a custom assert using macros, so you can have them trigger breakpoints in the debug environments, but write to a log file in release mode.

10.4.1 System Asserts or Custom?

Why don't you use the system asserts? You have greater control if you write your own custom asserts. For example, you can hit an assert and continue if you map your assert to a breakpoint.

```
1  // Define a set of custom breakpoints and asserts
2  #define DBG_HALT __asm{ int 3 }
3  #define DBG_ASSERT(exp) {if ( !(exp) ) {DBG_HALT;}}
```

For example, using a custom assert:

```
1  // Program Entry Point
2  void main()
3  {
4    // Example of using a custom assert
5    int val = 2;
6
7    // Assert test, halt here as val is obviously
8    // less than 10
9    DBG_ASSERT( val > 10 ); // Halt if val <= 10
```

```
10   }// End main()
```

When you hit the custom assert within the debugger you are instantly taken
to the line with the error You can single step through the problem, look in
the call stack of who called the function, or simple click continue and have
the program keep running.

10.5 In-Line Assembly

Often you should work smarter not harder. Very rarely do you need to go
down to the assembly level. While you can with C++, try and avoid it if
possible. In-line assembly makes your code platform and hardware specific.
Nevertheless, in-lining assembly gives you enormous power. You can integrate
in very low-level enhancements, such as calling processor specific instructions.

```
1    // Assembly breakpoint call
2    void main()
3    {
4        __asm
5        {
6            int 3  // breakpoint interrupt call
7        }
8    }// End main()
9
10   The 'int 3' instruction is defined for use by debuggers to ↩
         temporarily replace an instruction in a running program in ↩
         order to set a breakpoint.
11   The opcode for 'int 3' is 0xCC.  The dedicated 0xCC opcode has some ↩
         desired special properties for debugging, which is useful to ↩
         know.
```

Chapter 11

Simple Games

Age is an issue of mind over matter. If you don't mind, it doesn't matter.

Mark Twain

11.1 Introduction

This chapter presents some very simple C/C++ games. The full game source code is included in the book - so you can 'type' in the code to create some simple games. Typing in the code manually is much more beneficial than simply copy pasting - as you'll get to understand each line. As you type in the code - if you make any typing errors, it will help you debug and evaluate what is happening. While the games are the skeleton components, they demonstrate basic logic states, update callbacks, and game structuring. The games only output simple ascii text graphics. However, as you develop a greater understanding of other API, such as, OpenGL and DirectX, you'll be able to embellish the basic concepts with additional features, such as, fancy graphics, animations, and sounds to create more immersive video games.

11.2 Tic-Tac-Toe Game

Without overdoing it with physics and graphics, we can create some simple games. An uncomplicated and fun example is tic-tac-toe. Tic-tac-toe (or Noughts and crosses, Xs and Os) is a traditionally a paper-and-pencil game for two players, X and O, who take turns marking the spaces in a 3×3 grid. The player who succeeds in placing three respective marks in a horizontal, vertical, or diagonal row wins the game (see Figure 11.1).

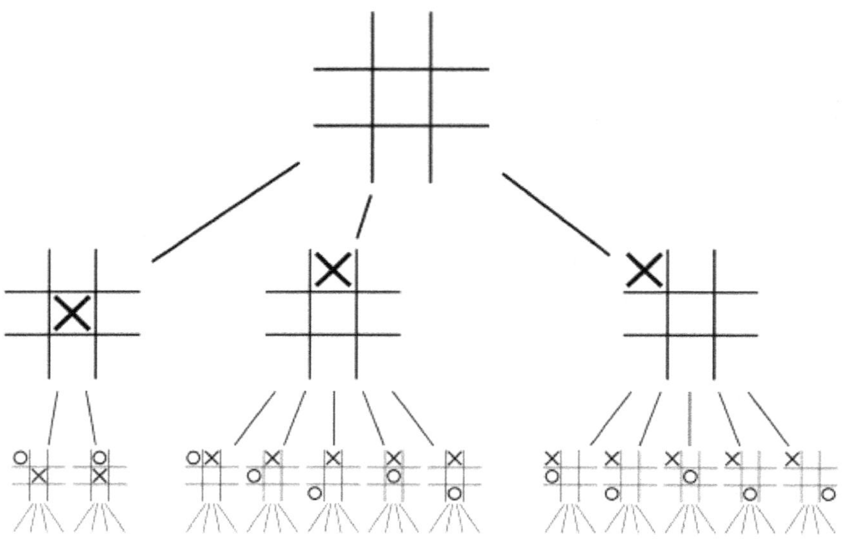

Figure 11.1. *Tic-Tac-Toe Game - Logical sequence of events behind the tic-tac-toe game.*

```
1   #include <iostream>
2   #include <string>
3
4   #define GRID_SIZE 9
5
6   using namespace std;
7
8   void printGame(char gameGrid[]);
9   void inputToSlot(char gameGrid[], int slot, char choice);
10  void initialiseGame(char gameGrid[]);
11  bool isFull(char gameGrid[]);
12  bool isEmpty(char input);
13  bool checkWon(char gameGrid[]);
14  bool rowWon(char gameGrid[]);
15  bool columnWon(char gameGrid[]);
16  bool diagonalWon(char gameGrid[]);
```

```cpp
17
18  int main(int argc, const char * argv[])
19  {
20      char gameGrid[GRID_SIZE];
21      initialiseGame(gameGrid);
22      int currentTurn = 0;
23
24      cout << "Tic Tac Toe" << endl << endl;
25      printGame(gameGrid);
26      cout << endl;
27
28      while (!isFull(gameGrid)) {
29          int slotChoice;
30          currentTurn += 1;
31          bool isP2 (currentTurn % 2 == 0);
32
33          // Prompt
34          if (isP2) {
35              cout << "Player 2 turn..." << endl << "Insert to slot > ←
    ";
36          } else {
37              cout << "Player 1 turn..." << endl << "Insert to slot > ←
    ";
38          }
39          cin >> slotChoice;
40
41          while (!isEmpty(gameGrid[slotChoice])) {
42              cout << "Slot occupied. Please select another slot > ";
43              cin >> slotChoice;
44          }
45
46          // Insert
47          if (isP2) {
48              gameGrid[slotChoice] = 'o';
49          } else {
50              gameGrid[slotChoice] = 'x';
51          }
52
53          // Print
54          printGame(gameGrid);
55          cout << endl;
56
57          // Check Winner
58          if (checkWon(gameGrid)) {
59              if (isP2) {
60                  cout << "Player 2 won the game.";
61              } else {
62                  cout << "Player 1 won the game.";
63              }
64
65              break;
66          }
67
68      }
69
70      if (!checkWon(gameGrid)) {
71          cout << "Draw.";
72      }
73
74
75  }
76
77  void initialiseGame(char gameGrid[]) {
```

```cpp
78      for (int i = 0; i < GRID_SIZE; ++i) {
79          gameGrid[i] = ' ';
80      }
81  }
82
83  void printGame(char gameGrid[]) {
84      cout << "+---+---+---+" << endl;
85      for (int i = 0; i < GRID_SIZE; ++i) {
86          cout << "| " << gameGrid[i] << " ";
87          if ((i+1) % 3 == 0 && i != 0) {
88              cout << "|" << endl;
89              cout << "+---+---+---+" << endl;
90          }
91      }
92  }
93
94  void inputToSlot(char gameGrid[], int slot, char choice) {
95      gameGrid[slot] = choice;
96
97  }
98
99  bool isFull(char gameGrid[]) {
100      for (int i = 0; i < GRID_SIZE; ++i) {
101          if (gameGrid[i] == ' ') {
102              return false;
103          }
104      }
105
106      return true;
107  }
108
109  bool isEmpty(char input) {
110      if (input == ' '){
111          return true;
112      }
113      return false;
114  }
115
116  bool checkWon(char gameGrid[]) {
117      if (rowWon(gameGrid)) {
118          return true;
119      } else if (columnWon(gameGrid)) {
120          return true;
121      } else if (diagonalWon(gameGrid)) {
122          return true;
123      }
124
125      return false;
126  }
127
128  bool rowWon(char gameGrid[]) {
129      for (int i = 0; i < GRID_SIZE; i += 3) {
130          char firstInRow = gameGrid[i];
131          char secondInRow = gameGrid[i + 1];
132          char thirdInRow = gameGrid[i + 2];
133
134          if (!isEmpty(firstInRow) && !isEmpty(secondInRow) && !←
      isEmpty(thirdInRow)) {
135              if (firstInRow == secondInRow && firstInRow == ←
      thirdInRow) {
136                  return true;
137              }
```

```
138            }
139        }
140
141        return false;
142 }
143
144 bool columnWon(char gameGrid[]) {
145        for (int i = 0; i < 3; ++i) {
146            char firstInColumn = gameGrid[i];
147            char secondInColumn = gameGrid[i + 3];
148            char thirdInColumn = gameGrid[i + 6];
149
150            if (!isEmpty(firstInColumn) && !isEmpty(secondInColumn) && !↩
        isEmpty(thirdInColumn)) {
151                if (firstInColumn == secondInColumn && firstInColumn == ↩
        thirdInColumn) {
152                    return true;
153                }
154            }
155
156        }
157
158        return false;
159 }
160
161 bool diagonalWon(char gameGrid[]) {
162        char center = gameGrid[4];
163        if (!isEmpty(center) && !isEmpty(gameGrid[0]) && !isEmpty(↩
        gameGrid[8])) {
164            if (center == gameGrid[0] && center == gameGrid[8]) {
165                return true;
166            }
167        } else if (!isEmpty(center) && !isEmpty(gameGrid[2]) && !isEmpty↩
        (gameGrid[6])) {
168            if (center == gameGrid[2] && center == gameGrid[6]) {
169                return true;
170            }
171        }
172
173        return false;
174
175 }
176
177
178 /***********************
179
180  Tic Tac Toe
181 Text Graphics
182
183  +---+---+---+
184  | x | o | x |
185  +---+---+---+
186  | x | o | x |
187  +---+---+---+
188  | o | o | x |
189  +---+---+---+
190
191 ***********************/
```

Listing 11.1. Basic Tic-Tac-Toe Game

11.3 Dice Rolling Game

An uncomplicated dice rolling game is given below in Listing 11.2.

```
1
2   #include<iostream>
3   #include<conio.h>
4   #include<time.h>
5   #include<stdlib.h>
6   #include <stdio.h>
7   #include <Windows.h>
8
9   using namespace std;
10
11  // forward declarations
12  void call();
13  void one();
14  void two();
15  void three();
16  void four();
17  void five();
18  void six();
19  void call();
20
21  // program entry point
22  int main()
23  {
24    cout<<"\n\n\n\n\t\Game: Dice Rolling Game.\n\t\tGuess and Roll.\n\←
        t\t" ;
25    cout<<"\n\n\t\tLoading. . . . . . ";
26    Sleep(3000);
27    cout<<"\n\n\t\tPress r to roll or q to quit the game "<<endl;
28    char ch;
29    ch = getch();
30    xm:
31    if (ch=='r'){
32    system("cls");
33    call();  }
34    else
35    exit (0);
36    cout<<endl<<endl<<"Press r to roll again q to quit!";
37    ch = getch();
38    goto xm;
39    getch();
40  }
41
42  void call()
43  {
44      srand (time(NULL));
45
46      int n;
47      n= rand();
48      n = 1 + n % 6;
49
50      switch (n)
51      {
52          case 1:
53              one();
54              break;
55          case 2:
56              two();
```

```cpp
57                  break;
58              case 3:
59                  three();
60                  break;
61              case 4:
62                  four();
63                  break;
64              case 5:
65                  five();
66                  break;
67              case 6:
68                  six();
69                  break;
70              default:
71                  cout<<"NONUM";
72          }
73  }
74
75
76  void one()
77  {
78      cout << " -----" << endl;
79      cout << "|     |" << endl;
80      cout << "|  0  |" << endl;
81      cout << "|     |" << endl;
82      cout << " -----" << endl;
83  }
84  void two()
85  {
86      cout << " -----" << endl;
87      cout << "|    0|" << endl;
88      cout << "|     |" << endl;
89      cout << "|0    |" << endl;
90      cout << " -----" << endl;
91  }
92  void three()
93  {
94      cout << " -----" << endl;
95      cout << "|    0|" << endl;
96      cout << "|  0  |" << endl;
97      cout << "|0    |" << endl;
98      cout << " -----" << endl;
99  }
100 void four()
101 {
102     cout << " -----" << endl;
103     cout << "|0   0|" << endl;
104     cout << "|     |" << endl;
105     cout << "|0   0|" << endl;
106     cout << " -----" << endl;
107 }
108 void five()
109 {
110     cout << " -----" << endl;
111     cout << "|0   0|" << endl;
112     cout << "|  0  |" << endl;
113     cout << "|0   0|" << endl;
114     cout << " -----" << endl;
115 }
116 void six()
117 {
118     cout << " -----" << endl;
```

```cpp
119    cout << "|O    O|" << endl;
120    cout << "|O    O|" << endl;
121    cout << "|O    O|" << endl;
122    cout <<  " -----" << endl;
123  }
124
125
126  /************************
127
128    Game: Dice Rolling Game
129
130    Guess and Roll.
131
132    Loading. . . . . .
133
134    Press r to roll or q to quit the game
135
136  ************************/
```

Listing 11.2. Dice Rolling Game

11.4 Ascii Snake Game

Snake is one of the all time nostalgic retro game classics. The concept requires the player maneuver the direction of the snake head which causes the snake segments to follow - each time food is eaten the stake grows in length. The player must avoid obstacles, such as the walls, not to mention avoiding the snake's own segments which are one of the hardest parts as time goes by.

```cpp
1   #include <iostream>
2   #include <windows.h>
3   #include <time.h>
4
5
6   using namespace std;
7
8
9   //console size: 25x80
10
11  //snake base struct
12  struct tagSnakeBody{
13    COORD snakePart;
14    char character;
15    struct tagSnakeBody* pNext;
16  };
17
18  class CTimer {
19    private:
20      unsigned startingTime;
21    public:
22      void start();
23      unsigned elapsedTime();
24  };
25
```

```cpp
26  void CTimer::start() {
27    startingTime = clock();
28  }
29
30  unsigned CTimer::elapsedTime() {
31    return ((unsigned) clock() - startingTime) / CLOCKS_PER_SEC;
32  }
33
34  //snake class
35  class CSnake {
36    private:
37      //snake it self
38      struct tagSnakeBody *pHead;
39
40    public:
41      //constructor
42      CSnake(int, int);
43
44      //global vars
45      int lifes;
46      int score;
47      COORD food;
48      bool foodExist;
49
50      //functions
51      void add2Tail();
52      void setCursorAndDraw(HANDLE);
53      void add2Coords(int x, int y);
54      void clearAllSnake(HANDLE console);
55      void setTalePositions();
56      void createFood(HANDLE console);
57      void clearFood(HANDLE console);
58      void detectFoodcollision();
59      void drawArena(HANDLE console);
60      bool detectAreacollision();
61      void resetSnake();
62      bool detectBodycollision();
63  };
64
65  //contructor
66  CSnake::CSnake(int x, int y) {
67    struct tagSnakeBody *pNew;
68    pHead = NULL;
69
70    //new Snake Head
71    pNew = (tagSnakeBody*)malloc(sizeof(struct tagSnakeBody));
72    pNew->pNext = NULL;
73    pNew->character = '@';
74    pNew->snakePart.X = x;
75    pNew->snakePart.Y = y;
76
77    pHead = pNew;
78    score = 0;
79    lifes = 3;
80  }
81
82  //adds a new bodypart to tail
83  void CSnake::add2Tail() {
84    struct tagSnakeBody *pNew;
85    struct tagSnakeBody *pAux;
86
87    //new Snake Body Part
88    pNew = (tagSnakeBody*)malloc(sizeof(struct tagSnakeBody));
```

```
 89     pNew->pNext = NULL;
 90     pNew->character = '*';
 91
 92     if(pHead == NULL)
 93       pHead = pNew;
 94     else
 95     {
 96       pAux = pHead;
 97       while(pAux->pNext != NULL)
 98         pAux = pAux->pNext;
 99       pNew->snakePart.X = pAux->snakePart.X - 1;
100       pNew->snakePart.Y = pAux->snakePart.Y;
101       pAux->pNext = pNew;
102     }
103
104 }
105
106 //Places the cursor on console at the same coords as Snake Head is
107 void CSnake::setCursorAndDraw(HANDLE console) {
108     struct tagSnakeBody *pAux;
109
110     if(pHead == NULL)
111       return;
112     else
113     {
114       pAux = pHead;
115       while(pAux != NULL)
116       {
117         SetConsoleCursorPosition(console, pAux->snakePart);
118         std::cout << pAux->character;
119         pAux = pAux->pNext;
120       }
121     }
122 }
123
124 //make it move
125 void CSnake::add2Coords(int x, int y) {
126   pHead->snakePart.X += x;
127   pHead->snakePart.Y += y;
128 }
129
130 //clears the last place where the snake has been at
131 void CSnake::clearAllSnake(HANDLE console) {
132     struct tagSnakeBody *pAux;
133
134     if(pHead == NULL)
135       return;
136     else
137     {
138       pAux = pHead;
139       while(pAux != NULL)
140       {
141         SetConsoleCursorPosition(console, pAux->snakePart);
142         std::cout << " ";
143         pAux = pAux->pNext;
144       }
145     }
146 }
147
148 //makes tale to move with the head
149 void CSnake::setTalePositions() {
150     struct tagSnakeBody *pAux;
151     struct tagSnakeBody *beforeAux;
```

```cpp
152
153    if(pHead == NULL)
154      return;
155    else
156    {
157      pAux = pHead;
158      while(pAux->pNext != NULL)
159        pAux = pAux->pNext;
160
161      while(pAux != pHead)
162      {
163        beforeAux = pHead;
164        while(beforeAux->pNext != pAux)
165          beforeAux = beforeAux->pNext;
166        pAux->snakePart = beforeAux->snakePart;
167        pAux = beforeAux;
168      }
169    }
170  }
171
172  //creates a piece of food at the console
173
174  void CSnake::createFood(HANDLE console) {
175    food.X = rand()%77+1;
176    food.Y = rand()%19+1;
177
178    SetConsoleCursorPosition(console, food);
179    std::cout << "&";
180  }
181
182  //clears the food if not eaten
183
184  void CSnake::clearFood(HANDLE console) {
185    SetConsoleCursorPosition(console, food);
186    std::cout << " ";
187  }
188
189  //food collision
190
191  void CSnake::detectFoodcollision() {
192    if(pHead->snakePart.X == food.X && pHead->snakePart.Y == food.Y)
193    {
194      foodExist = false;
195      score++;
196      add2Tail();
197    }
198  }
199
200  //draw snake arena
201
202  void CSnake::drawArena(HANDLE console) {
203    COORD auxCoord;
204
205    for(int i = 0; i < 80; i++)
206    {
207      for(int j = 0; j < 22; j++)
208      {
209        auxCoord.X = i;
210        auxCoord.Y = j;
211
212        if(j == 0 || j == 21 || i == 0 || i == 79)
213        {
214          SetConsoleCursorPosition(console, auxCoord);
```

```cpp
215            std::cout << "#";
216          }
217        }
218      }
219    }
220
221    //detect area collision
222
223    bool CSnake::detectAreacollision() {
224      if(pHead->snakePart.X == 0 || pHead->snakePart.X == 79
225        || pHead->snakePart.Y == 0 || pHead->snakePart.Y == 21)
226      {
227        lifes--;
228        return true;
229      }
230
231      return false;
232    }
233
234    //reset snake
235
236    void CSnake::resetSnake() {
237
238      struct tagSnakeBody *pNew;
239      pHead = NULL;
240
241      //new Snake Head
242      pNew = (tagSnakeBody*)malloc(sizeof(struct tagSnakeBody));
243      pNew->pNext = NULL;
244      pNew->character = '@';
245      pNew->snakePart.X = 10;
246      pNew->snakePart.Y = 10;
247
248      pHead = pNew;
249
250      for(int i = 0; i < 5; i++) //starts with Head + 5 on tail
251        add2Tail();
252    }
253
254    //detect collision with own body
255
256    bool CSnake::detectBodycollision() {
257      struct tagSnakeBody *pAux;
258
259      if(pHead == NULL)
260        return false;
261      else
262      {
263        pAux = pHead->pNext;
264        while(pAux != NULL)
265        {
266          if(pHead->snakePart.X == pAux->snakePart.X && pHead->snakePart↩
      .Y == pAux->snakePart.Y)
267          {
268            lifes--;
269            return true;
270          }
271          pAux = pAux->pNext;
272        }
273      }
274
275      return false;
276    }
```

```cpp
277
278
279  int main()
280  {
281    bool started = false;
282    HANDLE console = GetStdHandle(STD_OUTPUT_HANDLE);
283    COORD lastCoord = {0,0};
284    COORD scoreCoord = {3, 23};
285    CTimer timer;
286    CSnake snake(10,10);
287    unsigned foodInterval = 5;
288
289    for(int i = 0; i < 5; i++) //starts with Head + 5 on tail
290      snake.add2Tail();
291
292    snake.drawArena(console);
293    snake.setCursorAndDraw(console);
294
295    timer.start();
296
297    while(GetAsyncKeyState(VK_ESCAPE) == 0)
298    {
299      if(timer.elapsedTime() >= foodInterval)
300      {
301        if(snake.foodExist)
302          snake.clearFood(console);
303
304        snake.createFood(console);
305        snake.foodExist = true;
306        timer.start();
307      }
308      else
309      {
310        snake.clearAllSnake(console);
311
312        if(GetAsyncKeyState(VK_LEFT) != 0) {
313          snake.setTalePositions();
314          snake.add2Coords(-1, 0);
315          lastCoord.X = -1; lastCoord.Y = 0; started = true;
316        }
317        else if(GetAsyncKeyState(VK_RIGHT) != 0) {
318          snake.setTalePositions();
319          snake.add2Coords(1, 0);
320          lastCoord.X = 1; lastCoord.Y = 0; started = true;
321        }
322        else if(GetAsyncKeyState(VK_UP) != 0) {
323          snake.setTalePositions();
324          snake.add2Coords(0, -1);
325          lastCoord.X = 0; lastCoord.Y = -1; started = true;
326        }
327        else if(GetAsyncKeyState(VK_DOWN) != 0) {
328          snake.setTalePositions();
329          snake.add2Coords(0, 1);
330          lastCoord.X = 0; lastCoord.Y = 1; started = true;
331        }
332        else {
333          if(started)
334            snake.setTalePositions();
335          snake.add2Coords(lastCoord.X, lastCoord.Y);
336        }
337
338        if(snake.detectAreacollision() || snake.detectBodycollision())
```

```
339                 {
340                    lastCoord.X = 0;
341                    lastCoord.Y = 0;
342                    snake.clearAllSnake(console);
343                    started = false;
344                    snake.resetSnake();
345                    snake.drawArena(console);
346                 }
347                 else
348                 {
349                    snake.setCursorAndDraw(console);
350                    snake.detectFoodcollision();
351                 }
352
353                 SetConsoleCursorPosition(console, scoreCoord);
354                 cout << "Score: " << snake.score << " || Lives: " << snake.←
            lifes << "       ";
355
356                 if(snake.lifes <= 0)
357                    break;
358
359                 Sleep(80);
360              }
361           }
362
363        cout << "Game Over :)   ";
364
365        return 0;
366  }
```

Listing 11.3. Ascii Snake Game.

Figure 11.2. *Ascii Snake Game* - *Screencapture of Listing 11.3.*

Chapter 12

Beyond (i.e., What Now?)

Do not take life too seriously. You will never get out of it alive.

Elbert Hubbard

12.1 Truly Mastering C++

Only through lots of practical experience will you truly master C++. Always try to be open minded. Accept new and different ways of solving problems. Don't stick with programming rules just because that is the way you learnt to do them. Use logical reasoning. If you find a better, clearer, more flexible method, adopt it and move forward.

12.2 Graphics, DirectX, OpenGL

Video games and graphics go hand in hand. While you can output basic graphics using the default system API (e.g., Win32), for computationally powerful effects, you need to use, hardware acceleration, such as, the GPU (i.e., graphical processing unit). There are a number of ways of doing this. The two primary graphical method are Microsoft's DirectX (or XNA) and OpenGL.

12.3 Windows WinMain(..)

This book has primarily explained the basic principles of the C++ programming language, with platform independent libraries. While the program entry point is traditionally 'main', for windows graphical development, such as, Win32, the program entry point is 'WinMain' and takes an increased number of arguments. There is also a multitude of windows specific defines and libraries (e.g., #include ¡windows.h¿).

For example, without going into all the details, you can see the necessary bare bone code to create an empty graphical window in Windows:

```
// Windows common includes, e.g., WINAPI, HWND, and so on.
#include <windows.h>

// These are definitions which we'll define once here.
const char *CLASSNAME = "Win32 Example", *WINNAME = "A Simple Window←↩
    ";

LRESULT CALLBACK WndProc(HWND hWnd, unsigned int iMessage, WPARAM ←↩
    wParam, LPARAM lParam);

// This function is our program entry point, but this time its got a←↩
    lot
// of Windows initilisation code :-/
int WINAPI WinMain(HINSTANCE hInstance, HINSTANCE, LPSTR, int ←↩
    nCmdShow)
{
    HWND hWnd;
    MSG Message;
    WNDCLASS WndClass;
    ZeroMemory(&WndClass, sizeof(WndClass));

    WndClass.cbClsExtra = 0;
        WndClass.cbWndExtra = 0;
    // Casting, e.g. (HBRUSH), is for the compilers benefit, so ←↩
    that
    // it doesn't get unhappy, and to tell it that where passing a←↩
    paramter
    // but we want it passes as a HBRUSH or what ever we've cast ←↩
    it to.
    WndClass.hbrBackground = (HBRUSH)GetStockObject(WHITE_BRUSH);
    WndClass.hCursor = LoadCursor(NULL, IDC_ARROW);
    WndClass.hIcon = LoadIcon(hInstance, NULL);
    WndClass.hInstance = hInstance;
    WndClass.lpfnWndProc = WndProc;
    WndClass.lpszClassName = CLASSNAME;
    WndClass.style = CS_HREDRAW | CS_VREDRAW;
    if(!RegisterClass(&WndClass))
            return 0;

    hWnd = CreateWindow(CLASSNAME, WINNAME, WS_OVERLAPPEDWINDOW,
                        CW_USEDEFAULT, CW_USEDEFAULT, ←↩
        300, 200,
                        NULL, NULL, hInstance, NULL);

    ShowWindow(hWnd, nCmdShow);

    // This is our windows messaging loop!
```

```
40        while(GetMessage(&Message, hWnd, 0, 0))
41        {
42                TranslateMessage(&Message);
43                DispatchMessage(&Message);
44        }
45        return Message.wParam;
46 }
47
48 // This is our Call Back procedure, where you would put your code...↩
        this gets
49 // called repeatedly from our windows messaging loop.
50 LRESULT CALLBACK WndProc(HWND hWnd, UINT iMessage, WPARAM wParam, ↩
        LPARAM lParam)
51 {
52        switch(iMessage)
53        {
54            case WM_CLOSE:
55            case WM_DESTROY:
56                if(MessageBox(hWnd, "Leave? Quit the our mini ↩
        window?", "Message", MB_YESNO) == IDYES)
57                PostQuitMessage(0);
58                break;
59            default:
60                return DefWindowProc(hWnd, iMessage, wParam, ↩
        lParam);
61        }
62        return 0;
63 }
```

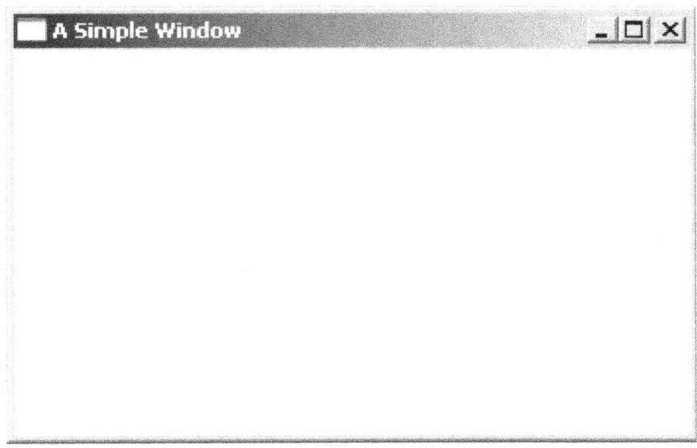

Figure 12.1. *Simple Win32 Window* - *Output from Listing 12.3.*

12.4 Video Consoles (e.g., Sony's PS4 and Microsoft's XBOX)

Each year new generations of console are coming out with ever increasing computational power. However, the system libraries and video games are developed in C and C++. Having a solid understanding of the language gives you a head start. Nevertheless, be expected to have to learn a large number of new libraries, specific to the console (i.e., the console has unique hardware that the developers want to use to give them an advantage over the competition).

12.5 Error Handling

Simple one-purpose functions should leave all or most error handling to the caller. This is more efficient because it eliminates error checking overhead on 'known good' input values. A common pattern is a low level function that performs no input validation along with a high level function that does (and then calls the low level function to do the work). Such a design pattern gives the caller maximum flexibility.

If the function must return error (or other status) values, it should do so via the return value whenever possible, and it should define an enum or type alias (typedef) so that the return value type name makes it clear that the value is a status. Note that using the return value as a status may necessitate extra arguments passed by reference so the function has a way to return a result to the caller without using the return value.

12.6 Signed vs. Unsigned

Consider this function: int CountWords(char* pszInputString);

The int type is a signed value, but a count is always zero or greater. The return value should at least be unsigned int, or better yet size_t: size_t Count-Words(char* pszInputString);

Likewise, arguments that must never be negative should always be declared as an unsigned type.

12.7 Pass by Value, by Reference, or by Pointer?

If the caller needs to pass arguments that the function will modify, they must be passed by reference. If the argument will not be modified, then it should be passed by value if it is a trivial type, else by const reference (except in unusual cases). For example: bool CountWords(const CountOptions& options, char* pszInputString, size_t& ctWords);

12.8 Const or Not

Incoming arguments that will not be modified should be declared const. This conveys a clear guarantee that the function will not try to modify the incoming value. Proper const delarations also give the optimizing compiler more ways to optimize the code.

Since counting words does not require the input string to be modifed, the CountWords() function's string argument should really be const char* const (constant pointer to constant char) instead of char*: size_t CountWords(const char* const pszInputString);

Now the caller can pass a string literal or any other string (even an MFC CString), and be assured that the CountWords function won't change it.

12.9 Exception specification

In C++, the exception specification conveys information about what kinds of exceptions a function may throw, either directly or indirectly via functions it calls. If a function cannot throw an exception, you should include the empty throw() suffix on the function declaration.

The Appendix

There's more than one way to skin a cat.

English Proverb

A.1 C++ Keywords

This is a list of reserved keywords in C++. Since they are used by the language, these keywords are not available for re-definition or overloading.

```
 1  alignas (since C++11)
 2  alignof (since C++11)
 3  and
 4  and_eq
 5  asm
 6  auto
 7  bitand
 8  bitor
 9  bool
10  break
11  case
12  catch
13  char
14  char16_t (since C++11)
15  char32_t (since C++11)
16  class
17  compl
18  const
```

```
19   constexpr (since C++11)
20   const_cast
21   continue
22   decltype (since C++11)
23   default
24   delete
25   do
26   double
27   dynamic_cast
28   else
29   enum
30   explicit
31   export
32   extern
33   false
34   float
35   for
36   friend
37   goto
38   if
39   inline
40   int
41   long
42   mutable
43   namespace
44   new
45   noexcept (since C++11)
46   not
47   not_eq
48   nullptr (since C++11)
49   operator
50   or
51   or_eq
52   private
53   protected
54   public
55   register
56   reinterpret_cast
57   return
58   short
59   signed
60   sizeof
61   static
62   static_assert (since C++11)
63   static_cast
64   struct
65   switch
66   template
67   this
68   thread_local (since C++11)
69   throw
70   true
71   try
72   typedef
73   typeid
74   typename
75   union
76   unsigned
77   using
78   virtual
79   void
80   volatile
81   wchar_t
82   while
```

```
83  xor
84  xor_eq
```

The following tokens are recognized by the preprocessor when in context of
a preprocessor directive:

```
1   if
2   elif
3   else
4   endif
5   defined
6   ifdef
7   ifndef
8   define
9   undef
10  include
11  line
12  error
13  pragma
```

A.2 Asserts

Implementation details for a custom set of assert macros. The macro enables
us to catch issues instantly - similarly, the macro can be disabled for final
builds or redirected to a log file to help track down difficult problems.

```
1   #ifdef _DEBUG
2     //#define DBG_HALT __asm{ int 3 } // or __debugbreak();
3     #define DBG_HALT { __debugbreak(); }
4     #define DBG_ASSERT(exp) {if ( !(exp) ) {DBG_HALT;}}
5     #define DBG_CHECKFLOAT(f) \
6     {
7       DBG_ASSERT( f!=f ); // NAN
8       DBG_ASSERT( f!=infinity );
9       DBG_ASSERT( f!=-infinity );
10    }
11  #else
12    #define DBG_HALT
13    #define DBG_ASSERT(exp)
14    #define DBG_CHECKFLOAT(f)
15  #endif // _DEBUG
16
17  // As libraries and classes evolve (e.g., vectors
18  // and matrices, additional tests can be included):
19
20  /*
21  #define DBG_CHECKVECTOR(v)  \
22  { DBG_CHECKFLOAT(v.x);
23    DBG_CHECKFLOAT(v.y);
24    DBG_CHECKFLOAT(v.z);
25  }
26
27  #define DBG_CHECKQUATERNION(v)  \
28  { DBG_CHECKFLOAT(v.x);
29    DBG_CHECKFLOAT(v.y);
```

```
30     DBG_CHECKFLOAT(v.z);
31     DBG_CHECKFLOAT(v.w);
32   }
33   */
```

A.3 Example Helper Functions

```
 1   inline float RandomFloat(float fmin, float fmax)
 2   {
 3     DBG_ASSERT(fmax>fmin);
 4     float r =
 5     (float)rand() / (float)RAND_MAX;
 6     return fmin + r * (fmax - fmin);
 7   }
 8
 9   /*******************/
10
11   inline int RandomInteger(int imin, int imax)
12   {
13     DBG_ASSERT(imax>=imin);
14     int maxRange = imax - imin;
15     if (maxRange==0) return imin;
16     int randInt = static_cast<int>( rand() / ( RAND_MAX / maxRange ) ↩
         % maxRange );
17     return imin + randInt;
18   }
19
20   /*******************/
21
22   template <typename T>
23   T Clamp( T val, T minv, T maxv )
24   {
25     if ( val < minv ) val = minv;
26     if ( val > maxv ) val = maxv;
27     return val;
28   }
29
30   /*******************/
31
32
33   // Saving debug information to the debug output window
34   // or a log file
35   inline void dprintf(const char *fmt, ...)
36   {
37     va_list parms;
38     // *Warning* be aware will cause a buffer
39     // overflow for very long strings
40     static char buf[2048] = {0};
41
42     // Try to print in the allocated space.
43     va_start(parms, fmt);
44     vsprintf (buf, fmt, parms);
45     va_end(parms);
46
47     // Dirty quick write the information out to a txt file
48     #if 0
49     FILE *fp = fopen("output.txt", "a+");
```

```
50      fprintf(fp, "%s", buf);
51      fclose(fp);
52      #endif
53
54      // Output to the visual studio window
55      OutputDebugString( buf );
56
57      // Output to the command prompt window
58      #if 0
59      printf(buf);
60          #endif
61  }// End dprintf(..)
```

Index